A GREAT

D1301356

A ROADMAP
TO SUCCESS!!

ALL
'S!!

## AN INFORMATIVE GUIDE!!

"Whether you're starting a business from scratch or buying an existing one—without a doubt you'll need *How to Be an Entrepreneur and Keep Your Sanity* to be successful. **There's no need to go it alone**—McCoy-Pinderhughes has laid out a game plan that helps you each and every step of the way. **Don't walk—run to get your copy** of *How to Be an Entrepreneur before they're all gone!* "
   —Sonya Donaldson, Technology Editor, ***Black Enterprise***

"African-Americans are less likely to start businesses than other ethnic group, partly because the entrepreneurial spirit is not nurtured in our communities like it once was. In *How to Be an Entrepreneur and Keep Your Sanity*, Paula McCoy Pinderhughes **demystifies the process of starting a business in a nurturing sister-friend style** that says to the reader: 'G'won! You can do it!'"
   —Cynthia Franklin, Editor, ***The KIP Business Report***

"**A MUST READ! Don't Start a Business Without This Book!**"
   —Terrie Williams, Author of *The Personal Touch: What You Really Need to Succeed in Today's Fast-Paced Business World* and *A Plentiful Harvest: Creating Balance and Harmony Through the Seven Living Virtues*

"Want to become self employed? **Pinderhughes, a former editor of *Black Enterprise Magazine***, presents a step-by-step process to achieving that dream, **covering such crucial issues as Franchising, Insurance and Banking.**"
   —Ann Burns, **Editor**, *Library Journal*

"Paula McCoy Pinderhughes' book *How to Be an Entrepreneur and Keep Your Sanity* offers advise with specific steps to invest in creative and sound methods to business ownership. **Before you begin writing your business plan, invest in this timely and informative guide.**"
   —Jesse B. Brown, Financial Expert and Author, *Pay Yourself First: The African American Guide to Financial Success and Security* and *101 Real Money Questions: The African-American Financial Question and Answer Book*

"McCoy-Pinderhughes gets real with *How to be an Entrepreneur and Keep Your Sanity*. She has provided the African American entrepreneur and small business owner with **straightforward advice, practical suggestions, motivating words and constant inspiration** to help you realize your dream. **This guide will save you valuable start-up time and serve as a reference for your continued success.**"

—Pearl Ridgley-Hopson, President, **InSight Development Strategies**

"McCoy Pinderhughes is one of the frankest and most incisive instructors on how to start a business. If creating and transmitting wealth from one generation to the next is the foundation of economic progress, then *How to be an Entrepreneur and Keep Your Sanity* is the mortar. **A fiercely intelligent and insightful author, McCoy Pinderhughes scores a bull's eye in her examination of, and challenges to, the would-be entrepreneur.** The result is an eloquent and enlightening playbook in a compelling trenchant prose that is a primer for newcomers and a refresher course for those who have already taken the plunge. **Entertaining, well-written and well-documented**; it is hard to ask for more."

—Craig Owen White, Partner, **Hahn Loeser & Parks LLP**

"Informative and well-written…**this guide will help you prepare, manage and succeed as an entrepreneur.**"

—Earl Cox, President & CEO, **Writersandpoets.com, LLC**

"**A great tool!** Ms. Pinderhughes has definitely written a book that provides a roadmap for business success. It covers all the bases."

—Jennifer Parker, President, **Black Capital Network, LLC.**

"McCoy-Pinderhughes gets real with *How to Be an Entrepreneur and Keep Your Sanity*. She understands the struggles African American entrepreneurs and small business owners face and has written a book to help them cut to the chase. **It's about time!**"

—Nadine Thompson, C.E.O. & President, **Warm Spirit**

"As a small business owner, I have given advice to would-be entrepreneurs that there are three key ingredients to starting a business; an understanding CPA, a sensitive banker and an aggressive attorney. Now, **I have added the fourth ingredient** (to starting a business)…*How to Be an Entrepreneur and Keep Your Sanity: The African American Guide to Starting and Growing Your Own Small Business* to the list."

—Marvin O. Smith, President, **The Marketing Exchange** (Monroe, LA)

# How to
# Be an Entrepreneur
# and
# Keep Your Sanity:

## The African-American Handbook & Guide to Owning, Building, and Maintaining —Successfully— Your Own Small Business

Paula McCoy Pinderhughes

Amber Books

Phoenix

New York    Los Angeles

First Edition
*How to Be an Entrepreneur and Keep Your Sanity: The African-American Handbook & Guide to Owning, Building and Maintaining Successfully Your Own Small Business*

Paula McCoy Pinderhughes

Published by:
**Amber Books**
**A Division of Amber Communications Group, Inc.**
**1334 East Chandler Boulevard, Suite 5-D67**
**Phoenix, AZ 85048**
amberbk@aol.com
**WWW.AMBERBOOKS.COM**

Tony Rose, Publisher/Editorial Director
Yvonne Rose, Senior Editor

Samuel P. Peabody, Associate Publisher
The Printed Page, Interior & Cover Design

ISBN#:  0-9727519-9-8

**Library of Congress Cataloging-in-Publication Data**
Pinderhughes, Paula McCoy.
   How to be an entrepreneur and keep your sanity : the African-American handbook & guide to owning, building and maintaining successfully your own small business / by Paula McCoy Pinderhughes.
      p. cm.
   Includes index.
   ISBN 0-9727519-9-8
      1. African American business enterprises--Management. 2. Small business--Management. 3. Entrepreneurship. 4. Success in business.  I. Title.

HD62.7.P727 2004
658.02'2'08996073—dc22

2004045791

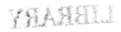

# Contents

# Dedication

*This book is dedicated to my sons Christopher and Justin, whose love, inspiration and willingness to sacrifice some of my 'mom' time helped to make this wonderful project a reality.*

# Acknowledgments

I want to thank the people who've stood by me through the difficult times, offering inspiration, believing in my God-inspired talents and encouraging me through their heartfelt words of wisdom. Just by your being, you all contributed to this book in more ways than I could ever express.

Thank you to my sister, Gloria 'Dottie' McCoy who listened to me go on and on about writing a book that would help entrepreneurs go from the idea stages to the real 'McCoy' and who often read countless pages and changes of a work in progress—we share a common vision of life. To my sisters Shirley Rowe and Pamela McCoy, thank you for always saying "We know whatever you put your mind to Paula, you will achieve."

And a special thank you to Tony Rose, Publisher & CEO, Amber Communications Group, Inc. I believe that it was God who made our introduction possible and for that I am truly grateful.

# About the Author

Paula McCoy-Pinderhughes is the former Small Business Editor for *Black Enterprise Magazine* where she wrote, assigned and edited articles for the 'Enterprise' (How-To) section of the international publication. Her contributions advised seasoned business owners on more efficient ways of running their enterprises while at the same time igniting the fire, providing the inspiration and sharing her business knowledge with countless entrepreneurs enabling them to begin the journey of realizing perhaps, a life long dream.

After completing her studies at Hofstra University on Long Island, earning a degree in Radio and Television Communications, she shifted gears and began her career with IBM as a systems engineer—later on entering the challenging game of marketing and sales. After more than a decade in the corporate environment, Paula decided to pursue her true passion—writing. Soon after, she published and edited the first African American newspaper, *The Franklin Voice* in her suburban hometown of Franklin Township, New Jersey for which she received an NAACP 'Entrepreneur of the Year Award' in 1998.

A writing career spanning more than a decade has allowed Paula to pursue and perfect her craft in innumerable venues. Today, Paula is the president of BCS-Business & Communication Specialists, a company specializing in writing and editing documents for small & large enterprises.

She resides in New Jersey with her sons, Christopher and Justin.

# Preface

How many times have you contemplated starting your own business and then put that thought on the back burner until the urge hits you again? You're not alone. There are thousands who insist that this will be the day to finally take charge of their personal and financial destinies—but only a select crowd who actually do it.

If you're among that special group of entrepreneurs who vow to take control and stand ready and prepared for the sometimes bumpy yet never boring road to business ownership and the immeasurable rewards that follow, roll up your sleeves and climb aboard, I've put together a book whose ideas and methods I've adhered to since the day I declared myself an entrepreneur.

Because we live in a society where the wealth of a nation is not distributed equally, we as African Americans, are obligated to ensure that not only our personal financial well-being is on solid ground through business ownership, but that we selflessly offer and leave behind the tools that will enable and extend to our descendants the ability to harvest the fruits of a bountiful labor.

Take this book and practice what I'm teaching—one step at a time. That's how anything is achieved—one step at a time—and when you encounter a glitch, don't give up, simply find another way around it or over it—but never, ever quit. Remember, there will always be a future generation looking back to see where you left off so they'll know where to pick up, and being an entrepreneur or small business owner is the perfect avenue on which to leave your lasting mark.

—Paula McCoy Pinderhughes

*"Each of us must earn our own existence, and how does one earn anything? Through perseverance, hard work and desire."*
—Thurgood Marshall

# Introduction

## On your mark—get ready—get set—Focus!

Whoever said life is full of unbeatable challenges could not have been an entrepreneur. And he or she certainly could not have been an African American entrepreneur. For blacks, life itself is a daily struggle from sun-up to sun-down. Combine that titanic effort with the will and desire to take control of ones own personal and financial destiny and the odds go through the roof. But what sets the African American entrepreneur apart from the rest is passion and persistence in the face of seemingly endless adversity. This passion consists of creativity, innovation, freedom, inspiration and independence—along with a driving endurance to succeed.

Like all other entrepreneurs, African Americans foster a burning desire and an unending commitment to making life better for themselves and their families through business ownership—seeking out interesting, useful, money making opportunities. And while we too enjoy a rich history of ancestral entrepreneurs, remarkable businesspersons who possessed an inner strength and displayed a strong desire to carve a patch into the quilt of financial liberation, these people encountered far greater strife than you or I might ever face. Yet, not unlike us, they were willing to stay the course until they achieved success. Entrepreneurs such as Madam C.J. Walker, the first black female millionaire, known for her black hair care products, to

Henry G. Parks, Jr. founder of the Parks Sausage Food empire. Even the host of contemporaries; Reginald Lewis, the entrepreneurial minded Wall Street dealmaker and former Chairman and CEO of TLC Beatrice International, Oprah Winfrey, world renowned entrepreneur, talk show host, actress, television producer and publisher, Bob Johnson, Chairman and CEO of BET, and Earl G. Graves, Chairman and CEO of Earl Graves Ltd., and publisher of *Black Enterprise Magazine*.

All have had to exercise patience and dodge racism on the rugged road to prosperity. But these entrepreneurs were and are constantly on the lookout for different ways to accomplish the familiar—exciting ways to reach a well-known destination. And although there will be those who don't always emerge victorious the first time, giving up when the many doors they must open don't necessarily have friendly faces waiting on the other side, true entrepreneurs keep trying until the gold medal of business success is theirs!

> *'If there is no struggle, there is no progress"*
> —Frederick Douglass

Now before we go any further, I have a few questions I'd like you to consider—to help sort through the entrepreneurial maze:

Where would you rather be at 6:00 am in the morning? In the shower getting ready to go work for someone else's dream or in your pajamas, laptop in hand, putting the final touches on your own.

How do you define happiness? Commuting for 45 minutes or more to Tyrone's House of Technology or is it working on your lawn on the weekend, creating a landscape that has ordinary people staring and your neighbors singing praises over your undeniable green-thumb talents.

Maybe your passion is taking pictures of your family and displaying the collection in a beautiful handmade album or capturing an inspiring sunrise or a romantic sunset through the camera lens. Is it that you're a devoted reader of black historical novels and feel an obligation to share the all-to-often 'elusive knowledge' with our brothers and sisters?

Who are you? A self-starter, ready to go at the drop of a dime? Or does it take a mountain of muscle to get you out of bed?

When you start a project, do you keep at it until it's complete or do you put it away for a minute, a month, or more?

Well, what'd you come up with so far? Does any of this sound like you? If so, let's go. I'm here to help you sort through the confusion and open the doors to entrepreneurial success. If you're not quite sure, read on, I think you'll find enough inspiration throughout these pages to help you make a wise decision.

First, let me explain how I've laid out the guide:

I'll assist you with the basics—things you'll need to do and think about before getting started. But there's definitely one thing you'll have to come up with on your own—and that's setting your own goals—you know, like why you're striking out on your own—and there are hundreds of reasons why African Americans make the move to self-employment. For some, it's because the opportunity for career advancement either never came or kept passing them by for lesser qualified or non-black employees. For others, the fear or threat of downsizing finally became a reality and they were forced out before they were financially prepared to leave. Or maybe the day finally arrived when facing that bigoted boss or petty supervisor for one more minute would have been irrefutable torture and the only rational thing left to do was to call it quits or mail in a resignation—leaving behind years of unappreciated experience and untapped skills on the employer's table!

The reason or reasons why you left or are considering leaving your job is something you'll need to always have in the back of your mind.

Why? Because those very same reasons will help you remain focused on succeeding when the day comes for striking out on your own.

In chapters three and four we'll discuss different business ideas and concepts to help determine whether this venture requires your full-time attention or if you can effectively start it part-time.

We'll talk about what you'd need if you want to start it from home or an outside building. You'll need to decide whether your personality fits the 'start from scratch' mold or the 'up and running' model. You'll also need to be aware of any laws or regulations requiring a permit or license in your city or county before hanging out the grand opening sign.

Have you given any thought to franchising? For some entrepreneurs franchising is the perfect solution to business ownership, so we'll touch on the risks and rewards of franchise opportunities. I'll even list some franchise options and what it'll cost to buy one.

And we can't afford not to discuss the importance of insurance coverage for you and the enterprise—something every entrepreneur should be savvy about. Remember, a responsible entrepreneur is always prepared for the unexpected.

Now a subject that most people might find intimidating is obtaining capital for their venture, money to help you start or keep you growing. But for the African American entrepreneur, the topic can seem that much more overwhelming, and frightening and all too often the actual experience, discouraging. I'll suggest ways to approach friends and family about investing in your dream, but if that doesn't bring in enough money to initiate lift-off, don't be afraid to head to your local bank for outside financing. Even if they turn you down, that could mean money in your pockets! I'll explain what I mean later on in the guide.

Listen, I'm here to tell you that you can get the money you need to start your business. It's out there. But it'll take guts, luck, and an 'ain't-gonna-give-up' attitude in order to find out whose 'got what you need!'

Not only have I talked to, written and read about entrepreneurs, many of them like yourselves, who had the dream but not the financial resource to get their venture up and running—I've been that person! And I'm here to tell you that the answer to any struggle is believing in yourself and your ability to make it happen—no matter what or how many obstacles there are blocking the doorway to prosperity. I'll pass along advice that was given to me by 'African-American friendly' lenders.

We'll touch on finding the right banking institution for your money. And let me emphasize, right. It's important that you feel comfortable with the people who are guarding your hard-earned dollars and growing profits.

And of course, what's entrepreneurship without the fun stuff like coming up with the perfect business name. But think about it before you put it on paper or on the outside of a storefront building. Give it some real thoughtful and meaningful consideration! Exotic or ethnic are fair game, as long as it projects the image you want to send to your potential customers.

Now I know you probably already have a couple of people you consider your best friends...folks who'll be there for you no matter what—they 'got your back.' Well, I'd like to add a few more to that celebrated list...I'll explain in detail in chapter 8.

Here's a question: What's a business without customers? Here's the answer: It's just an idea. So in order to give life to your fantasy, we'll talk about how to go about doing market research—finding out if there is a real need for your product or service, sketching out your customer base, (your target market), and carving a niche, (your individual specialty within that market.)

Once you've chosen your target market there are some crucial things you have to keep in mind—some of which are: Who else is targeting those customers—(your competition), how you'll spread the word about your business to that customer set—(through advertising), what image you want your firm to project—(branding), how you'll fund the business—(raising capital), what legal structure for the venture would benefit you most—(Sole Proprietorship, Partnership, LLC, 'C' Corporation or Sub Chapter 'S' Corporation) and someplace to keep all the answers to those questions besides in your head—(a business plan)—your roadmap to success.

And last but certainly not least, I'll provide a list of useful organizations that you're sure to call on for business help and assistance, government agencies that were created to make sure minority business owners get a piece of the pie, black business friendly banks, and informative web-sites, all of which you'll find at the end of the book as a valuable reference.

And the beauty of all this? I'll be with you every step of the way—closely guiding you toward that opening day ceremony!

Throughout the guide you'll find a sprinkling of 'Ask yourself questions' and 'Self checks' just to keep the 'entrepreneurial juices' flowing in the right direction. And I've taken the liberty of including some of my own words of wisdom—expressions I've come to live by that have sustained me through the difficult times and continuously inspire me to reach an even higher plain of entrepreneurship to this day.

Okay, now it's time to take a deep breath, roll up your sleeves, and cop a serious positive attitude…we're about to start a business!

The very first thing I'll need from you is a willingness and a pledge to accept and utilize information. Secondly, an eagerness to conduct invaluable research. Thirdly, some pure and honest soul searching. And lastly, a firm commitment to your dream. That's it. Ready? Let's go!

—Paula McCoy Pinderhughes

*"Entrepreneurs are simply those who understand that there is little difference between obstacle and opportunity and are able to turn both to their advantage."*
—Victor Kiam

# Chapter 1
# What Is an Entrepreneur?

A book definition of an entrepreneur: One who organizes and assumes the risk of a business or enterprise. My definition of an entrepreneur: A person who visualizes an idea or possesses a burning desire to make a change through hard work, dedication and determination, knowing that it will satisfy their ultimate personal and business objectives. Write in your own definition of what an entrepreneur is, right now:

_____

_____

_____

At the end of the guide we'll come back to it—see if anything has changed. Will you add to it? Subtract from it? Change it altogether or leave it just as it is. Whatever you decide, make sure that it's something whose definition and meaning will grow even stronger as the years pass by.

By now you should understand that entrepreneurship starts with a vision. A vision of how you need to make a change, how something you do, (a service) or something you have, (a product) can make yours and someone else's life much easier, gratifying and more fulfilling.

So let's start off by focusing on that vision and then take an inventory of the skills you have that can help you jump-start it into a real prototype, a model, but on paper first.

For now, let's concentrate on your skill strengths. We'll tackle your weaknesses later. And yes, you will need to own up to your weaknesses because whatever it is that you're not up to speed at will have to be passed along to someone or something else.

And keep this in mind: 'There is nothing to be ashamed of in admitting a lack of experience in a particular area.' On the other hand, successful entrepreneurs acknowledge that they stand to gain customer credibility, satisfaction and loyalty by looking at outside resources to step in when they need a specific skill.

Take a pen or pencil and write out what it is you're good at and what you like to do—personally and professionally.

Don't leave out your hobbies or your educational background. This is an important exercise—and it becomes even more important when you write it down. Think of it as 'visual confirmation'—a business tool you can later reference when laying down your business plan.

For example: you might want to categorize your list—as a matter of fact, I would strongly encourage you to do it.

Rate your skill strengths using a scale of 1 to 3. One (1) suggests being exposed to the skill. Two (2) suggests being experienced and Three (3) suggests being an expert.

## Ask yourself:

Mark 1, 2, or 3 in the box at the left.

☐ Are you good with your hands?

☐ Are you a people person?

☐ Are you a problem solver? (yours and others)

☐ Are you a technology genius?

☐ Do you love to talk while at the same time offering useful information?

☐ Are you artistic?

☐ Do numbers get your heart pumping?

☐ Does reading open up your world to unimaginable adventures?

☐ Is traveling something you couldn't stand to live without?

☐ Does serving up a delicious meal satisfy your friends and family's soul?

☐ Are you an animal lover?

☐ Do beautiful home decorations inspire you?

☐ Do people depend on your sense of 'where things belong' to get it all done?

The list is endless.

## Self Check:

Now it's time for you to make a personal list of things you could possibly do as an entrepreneur:

| | |
|---|---|
| ❏ Gardener | ❏ Travel agent or coordinator |
| ❏ Sculptor | ❏ Limousine Service Driver/ Owner |
| ❏ Counselor | ❏ Importer/Exporter |
| ❏ Personal Assistant | ❏ Pet Groomer |
| ❏ Party Planner | ❏ Interior Designer |
| ❏ Gift Basket Designer | ❏ Event Planner |
| ❏ Computer Specialist | ❏ Landscape Architect |
| ❏ Web Designer | ❏ Administrative Assistant |
| ❏ Artist | ❏ Pilot |
| ❏ Photographer | ❏ Janitorial/Cleaning Service |
| ❏ Chef | ❏ Exercise Instructor |
| ❏ Baker | ❏ Sports Trainer |
| ❏ Business Consultant | ❏ Advertising |
| ❏ Accountant | ❏ Career Coach |
| ❏ Tax Preparer | ❏ Construction |
| ❏ Financial Planner | ❏ Home and/or Business Security |
| ❏ Storyteller | |
| ❏ Writer | |

Only you know where your interests truly lie; I can only offer helpful suggestions. After careful consideration of your list, start to trim it down to the top ten, then the most likely five. We'll work with those.

I've always said that "Businesses are like snowflakes, they're all unique—each one should offer a new experience for the consumer."

So let's start to celebrate your uniqueness and make some money while doing it!

Once you've narrowed down your choices, on a separate sheet make a list of your weaknesses—what are the things that you would definitely love to steer clear of at all costs? And be very open and honest. Remember, we're working towards achieving your personal pot of gold.

## Take a careful look inside yourself:

Admit if you need some convincing when it comes to:

☐ Interacting with the public

☐ Organizing your thoughts as well as your desk.

☐ Competing on a daily basis to survive

☐ Selling yourself and your skills

☐ Managing dreaded business tasks such as hiring or firing workers, finding suppliers, manufacturers or delivery services if existing ones don't work out

☐ Giving up control—delegating what you don't have time to do

☐ Keeping the books

Can you add anything else to this list?

_____

_____

_____

Now let's compare and contrast your strengths and weaknesses.

Example: Maybe you love to travel but you're not exactly a people-person.

An on-line travel consultant Web-site might be right for you. That way, you get to do what you love and are skilled at without having the fear of interacting face to face with the outside world. This is an exercise that is crucial—take as much or as little time as you need. If you can't figure it all out right now…come back to it later.

## The Key to Success:

Be realistic and sincere. Keep in mind, this venture is an extension of who you are and what you'll be involved in each and every day. Be absolutely certain and up-front when it comes to your level of commitment.

*"The key to my success has been to give up everything for my dream."*
—John Johnson

Chapter 2
# The Golden Goal

Now that you've defined your strengths and weaknesses, let's re-examine why you want to venture out on your own. As I touched on before, for some African Americans, it's because they've been downsized—for others the reason stems from not being able to look at their manager, supervisor or forewoman one more day.

Maybe you work in the corporate world and you've reached the ominous 'glass ceiling'—what some call 'the end of the line for women and minorities.'

Or could it be that you've found the lack of respect in your workplace has finally led you to the door?

Still for some it's because you may have great ideas and no one really cares to listen or even value your opinion.

Or maybe the reason is simply that you're at the point in your life where you want total control over your time and finances.

No matter what the reason, you must set goals for starting your business.

## Ask Yourself:

▼ What do you want to accomplish short term? (weeks, months, a year) Is it Personal freedom?

▼ What about long term? (five or more years). Is it Financial security?

▼ Maybe you want to change your way of life—see more of the world or less of it—have more time on your hands or less of it.

▼ Do you want more control over your earning power? You feel you're worth more than what you're currently being paid.

▼ Could it be the thought of finally being your own boss that's got you all fired up?

Take your time and think about what your goal is and write it down. It helps to have an actual document that you can refer to in case you loose sight of why you've set off on this journey.

My Goal:

_____

_____

_____

_____

The most important exercise here is to think about your goal or goals and then think about it again. Whatever you come up with…stick to it…never lose site of it and most important of all, truly believe in it.

## Self Check:

▼ How do you perceive life?

▼ Is the glass half empty or half full?

▼ Do you believe in taking risks—even if it means failing?

▼ Are you determined?

▼ Are you willing to sacrifice your already precious, shrinking time?

▼ What about the thought of extended hours alone and countless sleepless nights?

▼ Are you ready for a challenge—even when you're feeling like the whole world is against you?

Pump yourself up mentally! This is an exercise that you might want to repeat every morning or once a week.

Here are some numbers to think about: According to the 1997 U.S. Census Survey of Minority Owned Business Enterprises (SMOBE), and the Minority Business Development Agency (MBDA), an organization committed to the empowerment of minority business enterprises, there were 823,499 African American companies generating $71.2 billion dollars in revenues. (statistics are available every five years). Most of those firms were concentrated in the service sector, (53%). The report goes on to say that four states accounted for 35 percent of African American owned firms: New York, California, Texas and California, while 3 out of 10 African Americans live in these states.

An estimated 24 million small businesses (minority and non-minority) are home-based. In 2002 alone, more than 365,000 firms were owned by African American women generating $14.5 billion in sales. Now although those numbers are encouraging you should keep in mind that according to the Small Business Administration, 50% of all new businesses fail within the first four years, and the numbers are even higher, 75% for African American businesses.

Among the leading factors for new business failures are:
▼ Lack of start-up and working capital

▼ Inaccurate estimate of product or service potential

▼ Lack of skills

▼ Ignoring the competition

▼ Bookkeeping mistakes

But as an entrepreneur this information shouldn't startle you, and it isn't meant to discourage you. I hope what it does is inform you of the real risks associated with business ownership and drive you to use this guide as the knowledge base you'll need on your road to victory.

These and other questions I'll ask you are merely brain exercises to get you thinking like an entrepreneur. You can rest assured that they'll come back to you time and time again while you're on your quest of discovering if you really have what it takes to be your own boss.

## The Key to Success:

There will be days when you'll want to sleep late or put off a task until tomorrow. Don't do it! Why? Because it'll be too tempting to do it again and again—don't do it! Find some words—a phrase, a quote or something I've written in the guide to keep you focused. You're not alone.

*"If you pray for only one thing, let it be for an idea."*
—Percy Sutton

## Chapter 3
# Sooo...What's the Big Idea?

Okay, remember that list you created in Chapter 1 contrasting your skill strengths with your weaknesses? Take it out again. By now it should be a short list. Look it over. Could any of the skills you have listed be transformed into a service or product? Think about whether or not the general population could use, or more likely, is using, a skill that you have or a product similar to something you've seen or produced. If it's geared toward African Americans how will that service or product target the niche market? Consider how you could or would persuade them that your skill, product or service is better, more efficient, or offers greater convenience than what they're using now.

How about what bothers you? Yeah, I know that we're all 'individuals,' but what annoys you may very well frustrate a lot of other people. Think about it. Take a look around your home, your office, your closet, your yard, or even your community. Listen to your friends, family and neighbors. What could stand a slight improvement, major repair or tiny innovation? "There's no need to replace the roof when there's only a loose shingle."

Think about your current lifestyle—are you pleased with it? What about the foods you eat? Are they healthy and satisfying? Look at the clothes you wear? Do you like the way you look? How about the way you or someone else styles your hair? Are you outdated?

Spend a moment providing answers to your own problems. You might just find that other people are willing to pay you to bring order into their lives.

Take another look at the short list of your skill strengths. This time, create a list of possible business opportunities alongside of it. The more possibilities the better. Don't worry about narrowing this new list just yet, that'll come soon enough. Don't even worry if the business sounds like something you've never heard of or seen before. Instead, take a good look at the new list and decide out of everything that you've written down, what activity would give you the most pleasure?

Keep in mind that whatever you choose will take patience, perseverance, time and self and/or family sacrifice while you're launching this exciting new enterprise. But it should also be fun. And I shouldn't have to restate that 'it will be risky.' Most good things worth striving for usually involve taking risks. But as an entrepreneur, I'm sure this is something you're more than already aware of?

Listen, I'm a realist, I know there are some African Americans who'll try and talk you out of seeking your entrepreneurial dream. They'll come up with all kinds of reasons for not pursuing it—such as: "More than half of all new businesses fail," "You're not thinking rationally," "Keep your real job and plan for your future retirement," or one of my favorites, "You're too old to start over." Now some of their proclamations might even seem, well, rational. But don't listen! Even if your initial venture doesn't pan out the way you want, don't give up! Never be afraid to fail! Try the next idea or rework the first one.

## The Key to Success:

Learn from your mistakes, stay tuned to your gut feelings and keep in mind that we take risks everyday—from the moment we wake up until we lay our heads down at night.

*If you get up early, work late, and pay your taxes,*
*you will get ahead if you strike oil."*
—J. Paul Getty

## Chapter 4
# Tick Tock-Tick Tock

The next big question is whether to cannonball into the pool or just dip a toe.

You must consider that even during a stable economic climate it's difficult for us as African Americans to just walk away from a reliable job—a secure financial base, which does after all, offer stability, a regular paycheck and important health benefits.

And it's very possible that you could use your spare time and weekends to work on your own venture.

I understand that ultimately your goal is to run the business full-time. But for now, you should carefully consider whether or not this is the best time to quit your full-time job.

Contemplate what your own real expectations about business ownership are.

If at least half of the following questions seem do-able, you sound like a viable candidate for starting a part-time venture.

## Ask Yourself:

| Yes | No | |
|-----|-----|-----|
| ☐ | ☐ | Are you financially secure enough to begin a business? |
| ☐ | ☐ | Are you mentally prepared for the challenge of striking out on your own? |
| ☐ | ☐ | Are you ready to give up weekend and evening family time to devote to the business? |
| ☐ | ☐ | Consider your evening hobbies—such as a game of basketball with the fellas or meeting a couple of girlfriends at the gym to relieve after work tension. What about that 'Thank God it's Friday' after work drink at the bar? Are you willing to limit that activity to once or maybe twice a month? Maybe even having to skip it altogether in the beginning stages of building the business? |
| ☐ | ☐ | Are family members on board with your plans just in case you need their help in setting up, shipping products or returning phone calls during the day? |
| ☐ | ☐ | If you have a full time job can you take advantage of breaks at work to accomplish an entrepreneurial task? |
| ☐ | ☐ | Is it possible to take some time alone during lunch to concentrate on your venture? |
| ☐ | ☐ | If you're a train commuter are you willing to catch up on some [business] start-up paperwork instead of catching up on some *zzzzzz's*? |
| ☐ | ☐ | Are you willing to adapt to new times and ideas or target a younger market? |
| ☐ | ☐ | If you fail at a task more than once, are you the type of individual who'll keep at it until it's finally accomplished? |

Now if any of it sounds too easy and you were ready mentally and financially to quit your job anyway, WAIT! Let's focus and talk about what you'll need to start full time:

First off, let's take into account all of the questions you answered above and whether they were positive or negative answers. If you gave positive answers to all ten, that's great, but you'll still need to be mentally prepared because there'll be a lot of late nights and early mornings (although they may be in the comfort of your own home or spent proudly in your new shop.) If your answers were mixed, (positive and negative) that's even better, because as an entrepreneur you'll want to be absolutely sure of what you're about to take on. Negative responses don't necessarily mean it's not a good time to start. They simply mean that you're being honest—and honesty is one of the greatest characteristics of any entrepreneur.

Next, make sure you have enough money set aside to live on before going solo. Some experts recommend putting away six months to a year's worth of living expenses. Everyone's situation is different. Realistically, there are plenty of African American small business owners and entrepreneurs who started out with one, two or three months of expense money stashed away. And, because of that fact alone, they worked harder and smarter and were able to get the venture on its feet—providing a sustainable operational income. Just take your time and think carefully about this. I know the feeling of being anxious about putting your idea out there as quickly as you can—before somebody else jumps on it—and it's entirely possible that you could do it in a relatively short period of time. You don't want and certainly don't need the added stress of worrying about how you're going to put food on the table or keep the roof over your family's head.

Explore the possibility of investors (family members and/or friends) for your business before launching. Professional investment firms rarely, if ever, loan money to start-up businesses. Community Banks are a possibility and an even greater one if the loans are backed by a government entity such as the Small Business Administration (SBA).

We'll talk more about how to approach banks in Chapter 7 and what the SBA requires and offers in Chapter 23. But as an entrepreneur you'll need to be able to show how much you believe in your company by investing some of your own money or collateral.

If you need to tap into your savings, do it carefully. Don't break the bank. Always leave yourself a cushion—the cold, bare pavement can be awfully hard. Look at your existing assets, things of value that you own. Is there something that could be sold and the money used to put into the business? For example, an older car that doesn't get much use, but one that a young driver might be willing to take off your hands and fix up.

What about that stereo equipment sitting in the basement? Is there a d-jay out there somewhere searching for those powerful woofers? Think creatively, but realistically. Never go in over your head. We'll explore more possibilities later on in the book.

If you truly want to start full-time but still have some financial reservations before becoming a one-person act, consider taking a part-time or weekend job until you reach your financial comfort zone. That way, you still have a salary for everyday expenses while still planning for and easing intelligently into the business.

Check your stamina. Think you can handle a part-time job while building an empire on very little sleep? No problem, right? Hey, you're not the first and you surely won't be the last entrepreneur to have tried it and then successfully achieved their goal on less than a full night's rest! The advice from seasoned entrepreneurs who've walked in your shoes is to make sure that you keep your health up. Bear in mind you're the boss, you can't afford to call in sick—besides, you'd only be calling yourself!

If you're married with children or have a significant partner, talk it over. They will definitely have to be involved in your decision. It's not one to be taken lightly because of the impact the start-up will have on you and your time away from them. The final choice of course, will be yours. But the impression will be far reaching. I always found it helpful to keep a timetable with completion dates. Not only did it keep me on track, it was a visible sign of progression for my family—they were always aware of when I was about to start a task and approximately how long it would take to finish it. (I've provided a sample timetable in Appendix E.)

Lets take time out for a self check and see how you measure up to your fellow entrepreneurs. In the years I spent in the corporate world as a marketer to small business owners and large corporate clients, I found there to be certain traits that were shared between entrepreneurs and executives. Look inside yourself and see if you can find any similarities:

## Self Check:

- ❏ Competitive in nature
- ❏ Harboring a never ending internal drive to succeed
- ❏ Persuasive
- ❏ Disciplined
- ❏ Sense of humor
- ❏ Understanding
- ❏ Stubborn
- ❏ Independent
- ❏ Able to make decisions and live with the outcome— whether good or bad?

- ❏ Confident
- ❏ Assertive
- ❏ Aggressive
- ❏ Humble
- ❏ Fearless
- ❏ Won't retreat at being told 'no, it can't be done'—makes you try that much harder
- ❏ Works well alone
- ❏ Always thinking about ways to improve something
- ❏ Quiet leader

Now don't be concerned if all of the traits listed previously don't describe you—as long as some of them do. Whatever you don't have can always be found in someone else. You'll also find a lot of those same traits in successful black executives running the multi-million dollar companies I mentioned in the introduction. It just goes to show that even at the corporate level they think like entrepreneurs!

## The Key to Success:

Understand the reality and the responsibility of business ownership—look before you leap! Make sure that the business you've chosen or are thinking about starting can make it through a changing economic climate.

*"If you don't drive your business
you will be driven out of business."*
—B.C. Forbes

## Chapter 5

# Home Based or Commercial Space?

The numbers are staggering. More than 24 million Americans have started home-based businesses. 2.5 million of those are run by African Americans. Nearly 1.5 million home businesses start everyday in the U.S. according to National Federation of Home-Based Businesses.

Now, we've already touched on some very important information but you'll also need to think about whether your business will be conducted from the comforts of home or whether you'll require outside space. Either location will require some initial examination. Of course you'll need more capital if you want to go outside your home. The decision is yours and not one you'll need to necessarily make today. Nonetheless, there are some things you'll want to consider.

I'm sure you already know that Apple Computer started as a home-based venture, and that firm is worth millions of dollars today. And I know you can probably name at least five or more others. But it didn't happen overnight. It took hard work, long hours and a strong belief in a dream—sound familiar? So before your company makes the cover of *Black Enterprise Magazine* or places on the Forbes 500 list—there are some checks and balances you'll need to prepare for.

## For the home-based business:

Some questions and suggestions to consider—

▼ Have you set aside a separate space for conducting a business in your home? (Maybe the basement, a spare bedroom, a rarely used dining room or even a revamped garage will do.)

▼ If you've already decided on a space—is it 'business ready?'

▼ Is there a separate phone and fax/modem line?

▼ Will there be someone there to answer your calls when you're away? If not, then you should have a professionally sounding voice mail system. (Don't settle for the bargain brand that's scratchy or one that might cut off a client or potential customer in mid-sentence.) This is extremely annoying and could cost you a sale or worse yet, your business reputation!

And when you or someone else does answer the call—make sure that you speak in your professional voice—using the company name instead of a rude 'Hello,' or an abrupt 'Speak.'

▼ What about your desktop PC or laptop—is it up to standard with the software you'll need to effectively run the business? Everything from word processing, billing and accounting to spreadsheet applications. You'll find some of them containing a little bit of everything in software applications or you might find that for now, you can use what's already on your system. But if not, shop around for the best prices and ask questions to make sure you get what you need in both software and hardware to properly run your operation.

▼ Keeping in mind that we're in an age of fast-moving technology, you'll want to consider having a Web-site. Maybe not the first day, week or month you open your business doors—but sooner rather than later.

Having a Web-site today was like advertising in the yellow pages twenty-five or thirty years ago—it's a very effective, far-reaching advertising tool. (Today it's as natural for a client to ask for your

Web-site or email address as it once was to ask for your business card or phone number.) But take the time to ask around for a reputable Web design firm or individual and make sure that you're comfortable with the end product result they're offering—confident that the site will coax customers to come to your place of business or place an order on-line.

As a consumer, ask yourself and others interested in your venture if the planned design evokes the effect you want as you go along. If you already subscribe to an Internet Service Provider, (ISP) such as AOL, Verizon, Earthlink or MSN, check to see whether they provide tools for making simple Web-pages for their existing customers.

Even if a Web-site is not in the immediate budget, you'll have to consider alternative ways of advertising: mailer coupons, yellow pages, fliers or local cable or radio stations just to give you a few ideas. We'll discuss the various ways to advertising success in detail, in Chapter 25.

## A word of caution:

Once you've begun your ad campaign, if you find that customers aren't immediately beating a pathway to your door—don't give up! Try a different means of advertising until you see some results—then stick with it for a set time. Don't quit after one or two weeks. Potential customers may not need your product or services right away—but if they repeatedly see your business name—when that time does arrive—who do you think they'll call?

**A true story**: I had just come home from a business trip and walked into my house only to be greeted by a foul smell. The toilet in the guest bathroom downstairs had overflowed and the carpeting in the hallway and the family room was soaked. I needed a plumber right away. The guy I'd been using for the past couple of years was not immediately available. So in desperation, I went to the drawer where I'd put the envelopes full of mailer coupons and found a couple of local companies. The wife of the first plumber answered the phone and said her husband was in the shower at the moment but that she could take my name and number and have him return the call—I declined. The company didn't seem professional enough. I really didn't need to know if the plumber was her husband and I certainly wasn't interested in the fact that he was in the shower! However, the second guy put me at ease and even made me laugh by telling me that I was the third overflow call he'd gotten in one day! "I think they know when you leave," he said, referring to the toilet, "and this is their way of showing objection, just like a puppy." He was at my house within an hour's time—and not only was the new guy quick and competent—he was extremely knowledgeable and friendly. So now, when I need a plumber or advice on plumbing hardware, I call the new guy first.

▼ Have you thought about an e-mail account using the business name? Check with your current ISP to find out if they offer multiple e-mail accounts, or shop around for a low-cost option. This would also serve as an inexpensive form of advertising.

▼ Have you chosen or designed your stationary and business cards yet?

Think about what might go on the card besides the usual—business name, address, phone number. How about your e-mail address, fax number, and a logo if you have one. If you haven't decided on a logo, most print shops will offer a variety of stock logos to choose from. But if you've brought in a sample logo created on your PC, or if you have some ideas in mind, shop around for the best printing price. Still yet, you have the option of purchasing blank stationary and business card stock at an office supply store and printing the business information on your own high quality inkjet or laser printer.

You might even want to try a non-standard size business card with information on the flip side related to your business offerings—but be careful not to make the card appear crowded with small writing.

## Always Remember:

Your stationary and business cards are a way for customers and potential customers to remember you. Be creative, not flashy, unless flashy is the image you're trying to project. Keep in mind, if you are targeting an African American niche market, your logo should reflect that market.

Find out if your city or town requires a business license or permit for home-based ventures. You may be subjected to an inspection of your work-space by the local officials to make sure that you are in compliance with building and fire codes. (It sounds more dramatic than it really is.) Fees for permits will range from $25 to $200 depending on where you live.

What about zoning laws? Can you legally operate a business from your home, condo, co-op or apartment? Check with your zoning or planning boards for specific zoning ordinances and your condo or townhouse homeowner association for any restrictions.

You wouldn't want to set up a successful business just to have to close it down because a jealous or nosey neighbor discovered your operation and reported it to the city, county or town administrators!

Spend a little time finding out what you need today so that you can spend a lot of time discovering what your customers want tomorrow!

Will clients be visiting your home-based operation? If so, a separate entrance from the main entrance of the house would be ideal if it is structurally and economically feasible.

Consider the image your office or shop will portray. Can you stand back and say: 'This place definitely looks professional and shouts: Open and ready to do business!'

Even your business address should be taken into consideration.

Let's imagine that you live on a street with a charming little name, a name that doesn't necessarily sound very businesslike. Or maybe you don't want to necessarily use your home address for business correspondence—you might consider renting a private mailbox within a nearby corporate park. Remember, image is important and an address in a corporate suite is more impressive than say, 35 Sunshine Lane—and it can make your small business seem as impressive as any business giant within the complex. Or, you could rent a P.O. box at the post office. The downside to that idea is that some customers or companies won't want to do business with a P.O. box. It all depends on the enterprise you've set up and how you're marketing the product or service. For some firms a P.O. box is all you really need. I published a community newspaper for three years before selling it and used a P.O. box for all of my business communication.

These are all suggestions—just things to keep in mind:

▼ Make sure that your workspace is always clean.

▼ Are pets housed safely and securely in another section of the home? You wouldn't want to have them greet your customers at the door, unless your business calls for friendly animals, like in a pet shop.

▼ Don't rule out a membership in a home-based business organization to network with other entrepreneurs, or just to share ideas or concerns. (You'll find a listing in Appendix C, the Business Resource section of the guide.)

▼ Consider forming partnerships for larger opportunities that you may not be able to handle alone.

▼ Make sure that you have a set time for getting started in the morning and take regular breaks. And unless you're 100% sure that no one will be stopping by—dress in comfortable casual clothing…answering the door in pajamas just doesn't project the right image to your client.

**FYI:**

Here are a few tax deductions you may be able to take as a home-based operation:

▼ A percentage of your rent or mortgage interest payments

▼ A portion of your real estate taxes

▼ Utility bills as they relate to your office space

▼ Furniture used in your office or subsequently purchased for your new space

▼ Office equipment

▼ Renovation and/or maintenance costs to get the space 'office ready'

Before taking these and other deductions, always check with your accountant, bookkeeper or tax preparer.

Are you disciplined enough to make family and friends acutely aware that the space you've created is really office space and that you're running a legitimate, professional business with set hours of operation? You'd better be—that's one of the qualities of a successful entrepreneur!

## For commercial office space:

Consider whether or not location is important. That may sound contrary to what you've always heard about where you live, work or run a business—"location, location, location." Well, where you raise your family and your proximity to work is a critical factor when choosing your living space, but for a business venture—it depends. It depends on what you're selling, manufacturing or offering in the form of services.

A commercial space within an office complex might be just what you had in mind—a location that could offer enormous potential for your particular business. You should, however, weight any obvious benefits against the disadvantages, such as set-up cost and rent.

Let's assume that your business is industrial or manufacturing. A facility with the proper floor plan, ventilation and utilities will need to be taken into consideration. A good rule of thumb here is to seek out the services of a real estate agent—someone that will help you find and screen out properties. A real estate agent is experienced in negotiating tenant or buyer leases and will work to get you the best deal for your money.

Now, before you go looking in the phone book for an agent, wait! I suggest you do some homework—ask friends or business associates for agent referrals. Talk to existing business owners in the area that you're looking at and ask for the name of their agent. Some will be helpful and some will not. The goal here is to collect a short list of names and talk openly with the agents—find out if they're experienced in finding the types of properties that you're interesting in setting up and remember, they'll be working for you, not the other way around. So feel empowered!

## Ask Yourself:

▼ How important is location for the success of my business?

▼ What are the 'geographic demographics' of your customer base? Example: Urban, suburban, rural or bedroom community?

▼ Will you depend heavily on foot traffic?

▼ Would a shopping mall provide the ideal space for your business?

▼ Could you operate from a kiosk or pushcart in an airport or mall setting in the start-up phase?

▼ Will you require a freestanding downtown retail shop?

There are plenty of details you need to be aware of before signing a lease. Leasing agreements will usually run from a minimum of one to three years and can be intimidating when you read them. Keep in mind that they are written to favor the landlord, but it's not impossible for you to negotiate the terms without the help of an agent or attorney. What you need to know is:

## The cost of rent

▼ How is that cost determined—by the square foot, etc?

▼ What amount of insurance coverage is required

▼ Any restrictions on hours of operation

▼ Are there any signage provisions? (height, width, size, lighting)

▼ Who is responsible for remodeling costs?

▼ Can a bail-out clause be included in the lease? (if your sales don't reach a certain number)

When it comes to retail space, the most crucial factor is visibility. Another is convenience and safety. Customers won't shop at you place of business if they can't find you and they certainly don't won't to travel for hours to reach you. And it goes without saying that your business location must be able to provide a sense of safety and security during their shopping experience.

Consider your future location requirements. Will the present site satisfy your growing business needs? You wouldn't want to have to pack up in a year because you've outgrown your tiny space. It's not a financially wise decision. By the same token, maybe your existing space can be expanded to accommodate your growth.

Another important factor to consider when choosing space, is knowing where the competition is. Are they near or far? Is that good or bad? If you're in the restaurant business you might want to 'cluster' with other like businesses. Customers are always looking for some place new and exciting to eat. Barber shops and beauty parlors have become more than just a place for a haircut and a wash and set. Nowadays, you'll find these businesses advertising themselves as 'full service salons' offering everything from a simple trim to a full body massage and makeover, and they could be located in large metropolises or sleepy towns, stealing the customers of the older shops who still only offer the traditional haircut.

Professional firms such as medical and legal offices tend to locate near hospitals and courthouses for obvious reasons. If you're offering billing services you might choose to be near the source of business, even if your competition is already there, there's always room for competition. Doctors and lawyers depend on quick and efficient billing of their patients and clients in order to get paid and oftentimes their in-house staff simply can't handle the load.

## When looking for the perfect location:

Keep an open mind as you check out the existing businesses in the area. Maybe your enterprise could benefit from them—maybe their customers will also need what you have to offer. Or maybe those very same businesses could become your customers too.

But you might still be wondering why two or more similar firms would operate in the same vicinity. Take the case of a business whose products or services are competitively priced and the only difference between you and the guy across the street is exceptional customer service or consistent on-time delivery of your product or service—guess whose profit line will boast larger numbers?

So, depending on your type of business, what you have to offer and how you present your firm, competition may not be a dirty word in your neighborhood.

You'll need to determine whether or not your shop is easily accessible. By accessibility I mean—will your business require parking facilities for customers or suppliers? Is your site near public transportation or major roads, such as highways, parkways or freeways? Is it accessible to the disabled?

Don't forget to ask about the history of the space—whether or not other businesses have been successful at this location. If some have failed, that doesn't necessarily mean that you shouldn't consider it—find out why. Maybe the problem was with the business and not its location. On the flip side, if others were successful—ask why. Were they similar to your shop? Find out why these firms either moved or were forced out of business before you sign on the dotted line.

Think about your need for employees. Will you require one, two or more? What skills are you looking for? Will there be enough qualified workers to choose from? Maybe you're not sure of what the going wage rate is in your area? For answers to these questions, start by contacting the local economic development agency and the Chamber of Commerce (See Appendix C).

Take a good look at the neighborhood. Is it a growth or declining area? As an entrepreneur you should never settle for a location in a 'changing neighborhood' with the promise of restoration in the near future. Your business may not be able to survive on a promise. If, on the other hand, the area has been designated as an Enterprise or Empowerment Zone, a depressed community targeted for redevelopment, offering tax incentives, lower utility rates, deferred construction related fees, speedier permits, low-interest government loan financing and creative marketing programs, don't turn your back just yet. These locations could be just what you, as a new business owner, are looking for.

## FYI:

Additional information can be found through the Department of Commerce Web-site www.commerce.gov, your local Chamber of Commerce, the town or city Web-site or from the Small Business Administration www.sba.gov.

Whatever you decide, be sure that you've taken the time to carefully research the facility and its location before making a commitment to your space.

As you can see there are a number of factors and plenty of questions to think about before you open the doors to success. But it's much better to work them out now than to experience costly mistakes later.

Right about now you might be feeling somewhat overwhelmed—it's okay, I know it's a lot to reflect on. But think of the information I've laid out for you like an all-you-can-eat buffet—there's plenty of food, so there's no need to pile it all on your plate at once. Go back later when you've had time to digest your first round. I've also included loads of helpful information at the end of the guide that will either provide you with answers or point you in the right direction to uncover them.

Take a minute to breath and stand up and stretch.

Now let's move on!

## The Key to Success:

Think long range. Don't spend more money than you have to because you foresee growth in the near future.

*Get the best people and train them well."*
—Charles Merrill

# Chapter 6
# Insurance

Let's talk a moment about insurance. Is your health insurance coverage still in effect? If so, great! If not, you'll need to look into what is available and reasonable for small business owners. Oftentimes trade associations offer group coverage at lower rates. Explore various options, including your local chamber of commerce, which might have information on area 'health-insurance networks' for small business owners. Also check the Internet for cost-effective plans. You'll find an extensive listing of African American Owned Insurance Companies in the Business Resources section of the guide (Appendix C) along with a national insurance consumer helpline.

## Did You Know?

There are several types of business insurance coverage:

❏ General Liability ❏ Malpractice Liability Insurance

❏ Property & Casualty ❏ Product Liability Insurance

❏ Worker's Compensation ❏ Survivor Income Insurance

❏ Business Interruption Coverage ❏ Fire & Theft Insurance

❏ Auto Insurance ❏ Umbrella Insurance

❏ Disability Insurance ❏ Business Owner's Policy (BOP)

❏ Life Insurance

What about business liability insurance? You have options here and it doesn't have to cost you an arm and a leg. You should check with your insurance agent to find out about attaching a business liability rider to your existing homeowner's policy. This rider protects you against any claims filed by persons injured while on your property or claims caused by the product or service you're offering or selling. Another type of insurance policy you should be aware of is business interruption coverage. This type of coverage will provide for lost income, overhead and equipment cost while your business is 'out of service' due to natural disasters such as earthquakes, floods, hurricanes, etc.

A lot of small business owners have chosen to go with a Business Owner's Policy (BOP). This policy packages a wide range of insurance needs including liability, property and theft. There are however, various conditions for home-based businesses purchasing a BOP plan—you'll need to talk it over with your insurance agent.

Being prepared for a disaster is something that every responsible adult should consider and as an entrepreneur that includes thinking about what would happen to the firm if you died? Having a life insurance policy will not only provide for your family, but it can also determine the survival or collapse of your business after creditors come in to take their share and the government looks for payment of the business' estate taxes.

If your firm operates as a partnership, a buy-sell agreement should be included in the partnership agreement. That way, the surviving partner has the option of buying the deceased partners share of the business.

If you're a medical professional, malpractice liability insurance is a must have and if you or your employees become disabled, you'll be glad to know that your disability insurance was in place.

I know you're wondering about the cost of all of this insurance coverage…and you're right to do so, but a good insurance agent will be able to offer you options when it comes to the type of coverage that's best suited to your particular business needs and the cost of various premiums.

## The Key to Success:

It's extremely important that you keep up your physical well being to be able to face the day-to-day demands of entrepreneurship.

*"Beware of little expenses.*
*A small leak will sink a great ship."*
—Benjamin Franklin

## Chapter 7
# Banking

There's no better time to get to the bank and open a separate account for the business than at the start-up phase. But, not just any bank, and maybe not necessarily at your present bank. You'll want to do some research here. If you've already established a good working relationship with your present banking institution and you feel confident in knowing that they'll provide you with the business services you anticipate needing—then, by all means, stick with them. On the other hand, if you'd rather shop around…let me lead the way.

### FYI:

You'll need to apply for a federal tax ID number that enables you to open a business checking account and file your business tax return, (something we all have to do as business owners). There are businesses operating as sole proprietors who use their social security numbers for tax preparation—which is perfectly legal; but if you have employees or you operate as a partnership or corporation, you'll need an Employer Identification Number (EIN). You can obtain an EIN by calling 1- (800) Tax-Form or through the mail from the IRS, www.irs.gov.

Opening up a checking account is crucial for conducting business with vendors or suppliers and you should do so under your name as

DBA or doing business as, (discussed further in Chapter 19) or under the business name with a tax ID number.

## Words of wisdom:

Never, ever mix your personal money with your business earnings, known as co-mingling. It's simply too confusing at tax time and you wouldn't want to send up a red flag to the IRS and risk an unwarranted audit.

The information you'll need to gather from a bank is whether or not they offer these services:

▼ Interest rates paid on your accounts

▼ Will there be holding periods on deposited funds—and if so—how long and can it be waived?

▼ What are the costs and service charges of a business checking account?

▼ Is there a returned check policy?

▼ Ask for overdraft protection on your account

▼ Does the bank offer merchant credit card services (use of Visa, Master Card, American Express, etc.,) for the convenience of your customers?

▼ Find out if ATM/Debit cards are available with business accounts

▼ Does the institution make loans to small businesses? (more about loans in Chapter 23, Show Me the Money!)

▼ Do they participate as a Small Business Administration (SBA) guaranteed lender? (discussed in greater detail in Chapter 23)

▼ Are their hours of operation convenient (walk-in or drive-thru) for your business banking needs

▼ Find out if they offer free notary services to their small business customers

Think about whether or not you'll need a credit card in the business' name. If you answered yes—get the details on interest and finance charges for unpaid balances.

## Interested in the export/import market?

The Export/Import Bank of the U.S., www.exim.gov, an independent government agency with financial products that include working capital loan guarantees and the issuance of credit insurance—enables minority and women-owned exporting firms to enter new markets and conduct business on shores other than their own.

## Minority friendly bank personnel are essential!

Although there are a lot of banks eager to service the ever-growing needs of a new venture, African Americans don't always find that their needs are at the top of that service list.

Before you deposit your well-deserved and hard-earned cash into an unfamiliar bank—talk to other African American small business owners who bank there about their experience.

Oftentimes you'll find that community banks are more inclined to working with entrepreneurs and small business owners than large corporate banks.

▼ You'll need to be up front and ask if the bank has specific policies and/or loan programs when it comes to servicing their African American business customers.

▼  Don't waste your time if the institution isn't willing to answer your questions to your satisfaction or seems uncomfortable in spending any time with you.

## The Key to Success:

The key factor in selecting a bank is whether or not they are willing to work for your business and how flexible their programs are.

*"The world cares very little about what a man or woman knows; it is what a man or woman is able to do that counts."*
—Booker T. Washington

## Chapter 8
# New Friends On The Block

Remember in the beginning of the guide when I mentioned adding a few new friends? Well, now's the time to reveal who they'll be.

### Lawyers

Your lawyer should be well-versed in small business set-ups. Why? Good question. Let me explain.

You might start your business as a sole proprietorship, but your goal is growth into a partnership or corporation. And with growth comes more responsibility and challenges. You'll need guidance from an experienced attorney to keep you on track when it comes to:

▼ state and federal government regulations
▼ business forms and documentation
▼ employee contracts for hiring and firing
▼ possible lawsuits that you may face
▼ collecting bad debts
▼ real estate transactions
▼ patent or trademark infringement
▼ issuing stock certificates for when you're ready to incorporate

In the beginning you're going to have a lot of questions, believe me, and you don't want to feel anxious about picking up the phone and calling your attorney, or driving over to the firm—so, what I'm saying is that you'll need to feel very comfortable with him or her.

One suggestion I'd strongly make is not to find your attorney through the yellow pages. I'm not suggesting that good attorneys can't be found in 'the book,' of course there are reputable firms spread throughout the pages. All I'm merely suggesting is that you start off by asking around—getting recommendations from other African American business owners or from your banker or from your other new friend, your accountant.

Once you've gotten a few names, you'll want to interview them. That's right, interview them. Remember what I said about feeling comfortable with your attorney. Ask them about a sliding fee scale for start-up ventures—or maybe they've developed a "legal package" for their small business clients offering a set amount of hours for a monthly fee.

Since legal advice doesn't always come cheap, I've made a list of options that you may find available in your town, city or state to help you make a decision when choosing an attorney:

| | |
|---|---|
| **Prepaid Legal Services Plan** | An option that lets you pay a monthly fee for routine legal services that might include phone consultations, contract reviews and written correspondence. These plans are sometimes contracted out by large firms to smaller firms and you may not get the same attorney when you require legal assistance. |
| **Legal Clinics** | Firms that offer services at a fixed-rate. Specific services will be offered at a set fee, for example: business structure set-up. But if you're looking for personalized, hand-holding service, this option probably won't offer it. However, the cost will be less than the services available from a private firm. |
| **Private Firms** | Costly for entrepreneurs, but you'll no doubt receive personal attention. |

Ultimately you and your budget will make the decision as to who and what type of legal services will fit your immediate needs.

Sometimes you find that smaller firms are more flexible than their larger counterparts. And as a newcomer on the business block, you can't afford to get lost in the shuffle of a large firm. I'm not suggesting that the bigger firms can't serve your needs; on the contrary, I know that they can and do service small enterprises everyday. What I am saying is that as entrepreneurs, you may have limited funds in the beginning, loads of questions and might require a little extra flexibility in terms of handholding, availability and cost.

## Did You Know?

Whether your final choice is a small, medium or large firm, I'd suggest you keep these qualifications in mind:

- ▼ The reputation of the firm
- ▼ A comfort level when talking with the attorney(s) at the firm

How they bill their time:

- ▼ Hourly—by the hour (or portion of an hour)
- ▼ Monthly Retainer—a fee that entitles you to routine legal services on a monthly basis
- ▼ Flat fee—available from some law firms that charge a flat fee for matters such as contract review or closing a loan
- ▼ Contingency fee—if lawyers are retained for lawsuits, they receive a percentage of the money recovered

When seeking out the services of a firm and conducting your initial interview, ask about the possibility of using paralegals to perform routine tasks. This will help to cut down your legal costs. Also try to negotiate certain fees with the firm. That's right—feel empowered, once again, to negotiate terms such as a discount of 5 to 10 percent for paying your invoice within 30 days. It couldn't hurt to ask.

Once you've made your decision on a law firm, you'll need your attorney to prepare an agreement also known as an engagement letter. This document will spell out the attorney's billing method and what they will do for you. Note whether or not you will be charged for expenses such as postage and photocopies.

A suggestion would be to ask for estimates before you actually commit your lawyer to a legal matter and to always be prepared before you pay him or her a visit. As an example, bring important documents with you pertaining to a particular matter, or better yet, fax it beforehand saving time during an in-person conference. And always know in advance what you want to discuss…keep in mind their methods of billing!

## FYI:

For additional help in sorting out the many services offered by law firms, contact the American Bar Association (202) 662-1000 or www.abanet.org.

## Accountants

Let's spend a couple of minutes discussing the financial health of your new firm. Now, I'm sure you can keep the family finances in check every month, never having to pay a late fee on credit card balances, rent or mortgage payments or school tuition. But managing your business finances requires a lot more discipline and understanding and it can become very complex, no matter how competent you are or the size of your new venture. And you may even find that you'd rather farm out routine tasks such as billing and payroll so that you can concentrate more on the growth of your firm. Well, the person that can assist you with that and other financial responsibilities is an accountant.

Earlier we discussed the importance of health and business insurance as a way of keeping yourself fit and your company safe. Now's the time to check the endurance of your firm—the financial endurance. Your accountant will be the one to assist you with this.

From the start-up phase to the corporate stage, accountants help keep businesses aware of where they stand financially at any given point in time.

For those entrepreneurs with a finance background, right about now you're probably saying 'I can do that for myself.' And to you I reply, 'More power to you.' But for the majority of people who have trouble reconciling their own personal checkbooks, there's help and the cost doesn't have to bankrupt you.

Of course there are software packages on the market that can help you with routine accounting functions (see Appendix B: Financial Resources for a list of popular brands), but a real live accountant offers more than just number crunching. You might seek out the services of an accountant to help you prepare financial statements for a loan, or advise you on cutting the cost of doing business, or inform you of the many tax breaks afforded to home-based ventures.

## FYI:

Here is a list of accounting offerings:

▼ Record keeping

▼ Tax planning and advice

▼ Auditing

▼ Year end financial statements

▼ Financial planning

▼ Invoicing

▼ Payroll

▼ Employee record keeping

This list comprises just some of the services accountants have to offer. And just like I suggested for lawyers, you need to ask around for recommendations, interview a couple of prospective candidates and negotiate the cost.

Some small business owners start off by using the services of a book-keeper for keeping the books (they're not as costly), then meet with their accountant prior to tax time, which is perfectly okay. Those bookkeeping services might include help with initially setting up your accounting system, tracking cash flow and preparation of income statements and balance sheets.

Other small business owners purchase software such as: Peachtree Complete Accounting, MYOB, Microsoft Small Business Manager and QuickBooks to perform the bookkeeping tasks listed above in addition to check printing, bank account and credit card records, generate monthly income and expense reports and much more.

Still others find that they would rather have a professional, someone who practices accounting day and night to take care of the financial aspect of their entrepreneurial endeavor.

More than likely you've seen ads offering the services of an accountant and other ads offering the services of a CPA (Certified Public Accountant.) The difference between accountants and CPA's is that CPA's are required to pass a rigorous two-day national exam and each CPA must be licensed by the state board of accountancy. Most states require a postgraduate degree.

Accountants don't have the same stringent requirements. However, most small business owners will not need CPA services until they are seeking investors. No matter who or what you choose for your record keeping and accounting needs, as the business owner, you should always be aware of the financial stability of your firm.

## The Key to Success:

You'll definitely need a knowledgeable lawyer and a competent accountant.

*"The road to success runs uphill."*
—Willie Davis

## Chapter 9
# From the Ground Up or Ready To Go?

Maybe you're one of those entrepreneurs who has already confidently made the decision to start a business from scratch, out of your home.

Then again, maybe you're the type of person who enjoys toying around with the idea of buying an already existing enterprise. Maybe you're the inquisitive type, investigating the sea of franchising opportunities.

Well, we touched upon home-based businesses way back in Chapter 5. So for now, lets take a look at the latter two and examine what each one would require—and hopefully by the time you finish reading this section, you'll be one step closer to a decision!

## Up and Running

What are the first steps you'd take in exploring a business to buy? Some entrepreneurs go to the classifieds section of the local newspaper and look under Business Opportunities or Businesses for Sale. There you might find a sizable listing.

Others can be found through industry trade associations or talking to business owners in the area you've chosen to set up your firm.

For some lucky entrepreneurs, buying an existing business means instant success—especially if the business has been operational for some time; enjoying a wide reaching positive reputation along with a firmly established customer base, knowledgeable employees; cash flow flowing in the right direction and unstoppable profits rolling through the door.

There are even instances where you'll find a business owner willing to finance the sale at a lower interest rate than a bank. Sound too good to be true? It's not. It is entirely possible to purchase such a business.

What's the catch? Cost. Existing businesses tend to require more up front cash than starting from scratch and you have to be absolutely sure whether that business is the right one for you.

## Ask Yourself:

Ask yourself all of the questions you asked when thinking about starting a home-based or commercial space venture—then add these on for size:

▼ What type of business would I like to own that would compliment and utilize my existing skills and previous working experience?

▼ Where would the perfect location for this business be?

▼ What size business would I feel comfortable operating?

▼ Can I search for an existing business on my own or do I need to recruit the services of a business broker? (Hiring a business broker would mean more of an initial cash output. Typically they charge a commission of five to ten percent of the purchase price of the business, but their experience and negotiating skills could far outweigh the costs.)

▼ How will the business be financed?

Always consider why the business is for sale and check with the Better Business Bureau for any registered complaints against the company or its owner. Hiring a security company to do a thorough background check and an appraiser to validate the value of the business would be a wise decision as well.

## Business Valuation

The following can be of help when it comes to business valuation.

- ▼ American Society of Appraisers at 1(800) 272-8258 (www.appraisers.org)
- ▼ Institute of Business Appraisers at (www.go-iba.org)
- ▼ Valuation Resources at (www.valuationresources.com)
- ▼ International Society of Appraisers (www.isa-appraisers.org)

The fees for such services vary, so be sure to inquire before committing.

Get your lawyer and accountant involved to do a more thorough search:

- ▼ Your lawyer will need to make certain that there are no liens against the property or legal liabilities pending.

- ▼ Your accountant will need access to income statements, balance sheets, cash flow statements and tax records for the past three to five years to determine the overall financial stability of the business before you sign the final papers.

If you are purchasing the business owners assets, i.e.: equipment, furniture, inventory or accounts receivable, you need to know if any of it has been pledged as collateral for prior debts.

The legal and financial assessment of the business is an exhausting task and will require time, due diligence and patience.

## The Key to Success:

It's better to take the time now rather than spend lots of time and money later trying to get out of a costly mistake.

*"I got my start by giving myself a start."*
—Madame CJ Walker

# Chapter 10
# Franchising

If buying an existing business or starting from scratch sounds like something you'd rather not tackle…then you might want to look into a franchise alternative. In a nutshell, a franchisee, (that being you), pays an initial fee and sales royalties to the franchisor, (the owner or parent company of the franchise). The fee and royalties permit use of a trademarked product or service, a proven operating system and consumer market packaged with training, marketing, advertising and ongoing support.

> **FYI:**
>
> Should you decide to go the franchise route, you'll be in good company. In the year 2000 alone, total sales of franchisees hit $1 trillion dollars! According to the International Franchise Association, (IFA) (www.franchise.org) there were 600,000 franchisees and steadily growing.

Owning a franchise will save you valuable time in your goal of becoming a business owner. A lot of the work is either done for you or the help and guidance is right there at your fingertips. Most of the mistakes entrepreneurs make in the start-up phases have already been worked out by the franchisor: Market demand for the product or service you're selling has been well defined and the reputation of the business is firmly established. You even have a choice of buying the franchise directly from the franchisor or purchasing an existing franchise, (already up and running.)

Now there's something new and exciting that has cropped up in the world of franchising in different sections the country: Home-Based Franchise Opportunities. This new concept allows prospective franchisees to get started with less than the initial monetary investment that is traditionally required. The International Franchise Association says that approximately 72% of franchises require initial investments upwards of $250,000 while home-based franchises can be had for as little as a $1,500 initial investment. This is possible because of the absence of high overhead costs normally associated with storefront enterprises and the high-end equipment needed to run them.

Of course no matter what type of set-up you choose, franchising doesn't come without its disadvantages—namely, restrictions on independent decision making and the way you would control your unique operation. There would also be a loss level of freedom to be your own boss and you'd have to conform to an established set of business practices and report sales and earnings information to the franchisor.

On the other hand, as an entrepreneur, you've already been made well aware of what it takes to be successful in the world of small business ownership.

You understand and are ready to accept the long, hard working hours, the responsibility of managing yourself and possibly others, the ability to multi-task (performing many jobs simultaneously) along with possessing impressive organizational skills. But in the end, the reward will be a realization of your dream with unimaginable personal and financial gain.

Aside from the fact that you'll bypass some of the hardships faced in the early stages, franchising is in some ways a safe alternative to the traditional method of starting and building a business.

## Did You Know?

There are three categories of franchising:

- ▼ **Distributorship**—granting the right to sell products previously owned by the parent company—example: car dealerships—DaimlerChrysler, Jaguar, Chevrolet—gasoline stations—ExxonMobil, BP Amoco, Hess

- ▼ **Trademark**—granting a manufacturing right to use a trademark or brand name in accordance to an established specification—example: soft drinks—Pepsi or Coke

- ▼ **Business format**—granting the right to sell the franchisors products or services and use its trademark and business methodology—example: food industry—Wendy's, KFC, McDonalds—car rental agencies—Hertz, Alamo, National

While the cost of a franchise is as widespread as the different types of franchises, ranging from as low as $1,000 to a high reaching into the millions, instant wealth is a delusion. Just as in most small business beginnings, the first year or two can be rough—bringing in little or no income. That's why it's important to do your homework before making a franchise decision and also make sure that you've put aside a little nest egg for the lean years.

You'll no doubt face some of the same challenges and concerns in franchising that you would as if your were to do it on your own: start-up capital restraints, scouting out a profitable location, certain risk factors and time constraints. But like any goal worth reaching, you'll have to weight the benefits against the obstacles.

According to the U.S. Department of Commerce, less than 5% of all franchises fail in their first year of operation in contrast to the SBA's calculation of a 50% failure rate for new small business ventures.

## Ask Yourself:

▼ Am I willing to run an enterprise where there are already set rules and regulations?

▼ Have I carefully researched and chosen a franchise that will compliment my skills and interest?

▼ Am I committed to staying with the franchise for the next 10 years—the typical length of a franchise contract? (some franchises offer a five year contract term)

▼ Can I financially afford the risk?

▼ Is your family on board with this time-intensive venture?

Depending on the state where you live and the location of the franchise, you may qualify for waived or reduced franchise fees. These franchises are typically found or must be constructed in an Enterprise/Empowerment Zone. Other franchise parent companies offer programs specifically targeting women and minorities.

Before making up your mind about a particular franchise, aggressively pursue what financial programs are available that could help you realize your dream of franchise ownership.

Now once you've made your final choice, you will receive a Uniform Franchise Offering, (UFOC) from the franchisor, which is equal to a disclosure statement.

The franchise industry, regulated by the Federal Trade Commission (FTC) is required to disclose such information as start-up and/or construction fees, operations cost and a detailed description of the franchise. The UFOC also contains information on any violations, pending or active lawsuits involving the franchisor or its executive officers.

Look for a list of current and former franchisees along with contact information in the document (I encourage you to contact some of them for a first-hand account of what it's like to own and run the franchise you're considering) and a sample copy of the agreement you'll sign upon acceptance into the franchise.

According to the FTC, by law, the UFOC must be made available to each potential franchisee within 10 business days prior to signing the franchise agreement. There are attorneys and accountants specializing in the sale and purchase of franchises...seek them out. You'll want to make certain that your interests are protected.

Here is a short list of some franchises you might come across on a daily basis and their parent company telephone number and/or web-sites.

## Home-based:

▼ Merry Maids, Inc.—(901) 537-8100
   (www.merrymaids.com)

▼ Lawn Doctor, Inc—(800) 631-5660
   (www.LawnDoctor.com)

▼ ServiceMaster—(800) 338-6833
   (www.SVM.com)

▼ The Home Team Inspection Service, Inc.—(800) 598-5297
   (www.hmteam.com)

▼ Colbert/Ball Tax Service—(888) 288-8675
   (www.franchisesolutions.com)
   or (www.colbertballtax.com)

## Traditional:

▼ Blimpie—(800) 447-6256 (www.Blimpie.com)

▼ Wingstop—(972) 686-6500 (www.wingstop.com)

▼ A&W Restaurants—(888) 456-2929 (www.franchise1.com)

▼ McDonalds—(630) 623-6196 (www.mcdonalds.com)

▼ Church's Chicken—(770) 350-3800 (www.afce.com)

▼ Midas Muffler—(800) 365-0007 (www.midas.com)

▼ Mail Boxes Etc.—(800) 456-0414 (www.mbe.com)

▼ Jani-King—(800) 552-5264 (www.janiking.com)

▼ Floor Coverings International (FCI) —(800) 955-4324 (www.carpetvan.com)

▼ Window Works—(800) 326-2659 (www.windowworks.net)

▼ Sign-A-Rama—(800) 286-8671 (www.sign-a-rama-com)

▼ OpenWorks—(800) 777-6736 (www.openworksweb.com)

▼ RE/Max International, Inc. (800) 525-7452 (www.REMAX.com)

▼ Jackson Hewitt Tax Service—(800) 277-3278 (www.jacksonhewitt.com)

And the list goes on and on. For additional franchise opportunities go to www.franchisee.org or www.franchise.org

## The Key to Success:

Like anything else, choosing a franchise takes the willingness to conduct diligent research and a strong belief in your own abilities to achieve success.

*"As a small businessperson,
you have no greater leverage than the truth."*
—Paul Hawken

## Chapter 11

# Size Doesn't Matter Online

For many small business owners, giving the customer that little extra something is what they must do to remain on top. In the world of business it's known as 'value added service.' But at the same time they must keep costs down while holding off the competition.

It's a serious juggling game. But in order to reach the 'ever-moving target' of profitability and growth, many entrepreneurs are turning to the Internet to do that and a whole lot more.

The barriers of a brick-and-mortar storefront are non-existent in cyberspace. Whether you operate out of a storefront or a home office, the Internet provides accessibility and convenience for your customer through what is commonly referred to as e-commerce, (electronic commerce.)

There, you're only limited by your imagination not your location. In cyberspace, size doesn't matter. Entrepreneurs can compete with the Fortune 500 crowd, and like them, your customer base now has a global reach. Your market potential has extended into a worldwide audience without you ever having to leave the comforts of home or the familiarity of your city or town.

When the time comes for constructing a web-site, it doesn't have to bring with it a soaring price tag. You can either build it yourself with available software tools, hire a local Webmaster to do it for you or find a company on-line whose specialty is Web-site construction.

Maybe your business is the type that won't require a 'physical' location. A company like Amazon.com, a bookseller and leader in on-line commerce, exists only in cyberspace—doing everything from order taking to order shipping. And the numbers prove that this sales medium is more than profitable if done right.

## Something to Think About:

In 2002, on-line commerce accounted for more than $35.5 billion dollars in sales, a staggering number by any measure.

Even if you're selling information and someone could benefit from using it—there's a great possibility you stand to make money from it.

Remember back in Chapter 1 when we discussed your professional background, skills, hobbies and education? You could possibly market your expertise or knowledge as an online consultant.

You already understand that as a new business owner, you can't be all things to all people and there will come a time when you just might need to call on someone else's expertise for assistance.

Going digital gives you access to experts who may not be immediately available in your area when you need them. Or it could open up new opportunities for 'strategic alliances'—(sharing resources and complimentary skills with other companies) making it possible for your firm to grow at a speed greater than it ever could the conventional way.

Routine overhead costs of employees or rent of a physical location is non-existent in cyberspace—but you'll still have the cost of hosting (paying Internet Service Providers to store your Web-site), maintenance and upkeep of your sight.

Ever hear of the competitive edge? Think of all the households in the U.S. and overseas who have computers with Internet access. Now think of those very same households as potential consumers for your product or service. If you didn't have a Web presence, those same households would be fair game for your competitor—but because you do, you are now a fierce contender to the largest, wealthiest corporations selling similar merchandise.

From the corner store florist to the Wall Street brokerage firms, having a Web address is as valuable and profitable today as a delivery truck and a telephone were yesterday.

## Self Check:

Regardless of whether e-commerce will be the basis of your entire business operation or serve as an extension of your offerings, there are steps you need to take to make sure that you're not here today and gone tomorrow.

▼ Have a definite plan for what you want to market on-line

▼ Determine if having a site is cost effective? Take into account design, marketing and maintenance expense

▼ Will it meet an unmet need for your target audience

▼ Are your products or services priced for on-line competition? You'll still need to make a profit

▼ Research the market for similar businesses. Are they suited for on-line commerce?

The Internet and e-commerce have opened up marketing avenues that were closed to small businesses 15 or 20 years ago. The playing fields have been leveled and the opportunities, endless. You may not have gotten in on the ground floor but the view from where you're standing can be just as profitable.

## The Key to Success:

A brick-and-mortar retail site is still the way most small businesses operate, but by adding a Web factor to the mix, you're able to satisfy the customer by making it easier to shop for products and services while reinventing your enterprise in ways you thought never imaginable as a start-up.

*"Always continue the climb.
It is possible for you to do whatever you choose,
if you first get to know who you are and
are willing to work with a power that is
greater than ourselves to do it."*
—Oprah Winfrey

# Chapter 12
# I've Got a Niche!

Once you've determined the industry you're interested in, and the market within that industry, you can narrow it down into segments and even further into a specific niche.

For example, within the publishing industry you will find book publishers, magazine publishers or newspaper publishers. Within the book publishers market you might sell children's books and from that segment you may want to target African American children. You've now narrowed your field to a specific niche within the book publishing market.

Creating a niche takes some effort. Learn to listen when people tell you they need something but can't find it in an existing product or service and then trust your knowledge, background and instincts to fill that void.

Once you've come up with a solution to the consumer's problem or concern you'll need to come up with a strategy for cleverly introducing it into the marketplace.

Think about this. If you're a traveler and you have an airport layover and you need to check your email, it's no longer necessary that you have a laptop with you equipped with an Internet connection anymore.

There are Internet Stations in many domestic and international airports today. So not only can you check your email, you can shop, check in with family and friends or play games to pass the time. Someone found a niche within the technology market and filled it.

> **FYI:**
>
> A niche doesn't have to be limited to offerings in the U.S.
>
> Look to other countries to find out what markets are being under served. (See Appendix C for a web-site on the export/import market.)

Creating a niche is what Sam Walton did in 1977 when he looked at a segment of the market—customers looking for quality at a bargain price and a pleasant shopping experience and created the Wal-Mart stores. It's also what John W. Nordstrom did when he opened Nordstrom's, a store catering to the upscale, fashion conscience, discriminating buyer. Both stores are in the retail industry, but each found a separate niche within it—a clever, profit-making niche.

Your niche, of course, doesn't have to be on such a grand scale, but I wanted to show you the microcosm within the macrocosm—the seed that grows into a tree.

Sometimes when you're thinking of a niche, think small, smaller, smallest. If you are targeting women—consider age, race, income and hobbies.

Let me spell it out for you: 25- to 35-year-old African American females making $60,000 and above, who enjoy reading romance novels. That's your market and your niche! Take a look within your own skill's database to see if you can find a market targeting that demographic segment.

## Something to Think About:

There are certain characteristics of most small business owners when it comes to niche strategy:

▼ They create or define a need

▼ They know customers want to have what they're offering

▼ They've researched and found that no one else has it or if they do, they'll offer a new twist or enhancement to the existing product or service

▼ They understand that they can profit from it

At other times think specialization within a niche. For instance, a shoe store that sells athletic shoes for men only. There are times when specialties can be advantageous—for example; you could sell running shoes exclusively in that athletic shoe store for men only. But be careful here.

Don't box yourself in too tightly. You might want to leave room for new niches that could compliment your existing niche—for example: hard to find athletic running shoe sizes for men, women and children.

In the following chapters we'll discuss market research and target marketing, a more in dept view of who you're selling to and why they buy from you.

Be patient, you're getting there. Soon you'll be among the army of entrepreneurs who go from having a vision to accomplishing your dream.

## The Key to Success:

Remember way back in the beginning when I told you that you'd need to focus? "Creating a niche is your focusing tool."

*"Get your ideas on paper and study them.
Do not let them go to waste!"*
—Les Brown

## Chapter 13
# Marketing Research

Marketing research is a tool that allows you to determine if there is a demand for your product or service. Will the public want or need what you're offering? Begin by talking to your friends and family and asking them for their wish list—what products or services do they wish they had that would make life a little easier or more interesting.

### Words of wisdom:

There will always be someone proclaiming to have built the better mousetrap—because the desire to improve upon what we already have is human nature.

Try attending industry trade shows in your city or town (some of them cost as little as $25 to attend)—they'll give you an insight as to what is being introduced to the marketplace. While there, you could get an unexpected bonus as your walk the floor and visit various booths—you could end up meeting with potential suppliers or future customers.

You might even consider creating a simple marketing questionnaire.

It's a good idea to conduct market research before deciding on a target market audience. Why? Because the information you gather will give you better insight as to who your consumer is. And it won't require a pile of money to conduct this research—it just takes time and determination.

## For Example:

Some of the information you'll want to capture from the public would be:

▼ Determining the need for a particular product or service

Example: Does your busy schedule leave little time for housekeeping?

▼ Customer profile questions

Example: Are you a commuter?

▼ Competition

Example: Does your current cleaning service do windows?

▼ Convenience

Example: How do you go about finding housekeeping services? i.e.: newspapers, placing an ad, word of mouth, fliers?

The data collected should be able to tell you if your product or service requires any adjustments or if you're targeting the right location for your business.

Tapping the Service Core of Retired Executives (SCORE) can be an excellent tool for assisting entrepreneurs with business advice, counseling and training.

Although most of the volunteers are retired, their expertise as former corporate managers, marketers, lawyers, business owners and financial consultants is invaluable and their services are free.

SCORE volunteers maintain a national skills database to match you with the right counselor for your business needs. Counselors are available in person, by telephone or on the Internet.

Depending on your immediate needs, you'll either have a face to face meeting, a telephone discussion or a cyberspace consultation.

This is one resource you don't want to pass over. Since 1986, I've consulted with the SCORE volunteers and the information they've given me has been invaluable and long lasting.

## FYI:

Service Core of Retired Executives (SCORE), www.score.org, or (800) 634-0245, a national organization of volunteers with more than 385 offices located in most major cities across the U.S. and funded by the Small Business Administration (SBA)

Take a trip over to your local Minority Business Development Center. The information and help you'll receive from the counselors is outstanding. Their knowledge and patience go beyond the call of duty when it comes to helping you structure your business plan, fill out loan applications and general business counseling sessions.

Mitchell Greene, executive Director of the New Jersey Statewide Minority Business Development Center encourages entrepreneurs to contact the MBDC and be ready to "explore the many options entrepreneurs and small businesses have when it comes to getting what you need in terms of financing."

### The Key to Success:

Do the research before you start your business. Make sure there is a need or demand for your product or service.

*"Business has only two functions—*
*marketing and innovation."*
—Peter F. Drucker

## Chapter 14
# Target Marketing—I want YOU!

Let's focus on your niche—that little place in the market that's all yours. Take time to define your market—it's not good to try and be a jack of all trades. You'll quickly face burnout and surefire disappointment.

Your goal in target marketing is to develop a profile of your customer based on certain criteria: Demographics and Psychographics.

▼ Demographics refer to age, income, sex, education, occupation, marital status, and ethnic background. The geographic demographic of the consumer, or where they're physically located is also important—including city, state, town, and community. Regions are equally as important in determining who you're selling to and how you sell to them. Consumers on the West Coast and southern regions may not be as willing to purchase a snow shovel as their counterparts in the northernmost or eastern cities.

▼ Psychographics refer to the psychological characteristics of your target market. The lifestyle, interests, values and opinions of the consumer are taken into consideration as well as political and religious affiliations. Buying patterns can be gathered from this psychographic exercise by determining what made one product more attractive to the buyer than the other.

## Ask Yourself:

▼ Are they impulse buyers or do they think endlessly before finally making a buying decision?

▼ How often do they shop—daily, weekly, monthly?

▼ Who am I selling to? Example: Are they 25 to 40 year old tech savvy males with incomes of $45,000 and up? Or maybe it's the college educated African American female in the 35 to 55 year old age range with a tendency to travel globally.

▼ What are their spending habits?

▼ Where are they located?

▼ Why would they buy what I'm selling?

▼ Are they willing to walk into my shop to purchase the product(s) or services offered or would they prefer the mail order or cyber method?

▼ What price are they willing to pay for the product or service?

All of this information will help you to understand your customer—your target market.

I've given you some critical issues to think about. However, the answers need not be overwhelming. They'll simply require some information gathering—either on your part or if you choose, you can hire someone to do it for you.

Of course, you always have the option of seeking help from a professional marketing research firm. However, doing so will cost more than if you conducted the research on your own or with the assistance of the organizations and institutions listed above, but there's always the off chance that you could barter your product or service for theirs. It couldn't hurt to ask!

To define your target market even further, you'll need to decide what segment of the market you'd like to sell your products or services to? Will it be to businesses (business to business or b2b) or directly to consumers (business to consumer or b2c)? Here's a hint. If your market will be selling to customers who will use your product then you're operating as a b2c—i.e.: retail clothing shop. On the other hand, if your customer will be purchasing your product with the intent of reselling it to someone else…then you're functioning as a b2b—i.e.: Goodyear Tire distributor. And of course just to mix things up a little, you could be a combination of the two, selling to both consumers and businesses—i.e.: Office Max or Staples office supply stores.

Now, once you've found the answers to all of your target market questions, established your niche product or service, and you're up and running—don't become smug and rest on your laurels—go beyond what's expected of you. Continue to test-market your product or service in hopes of reaching new and additional customers.

It's good to know that there's always free or nominal fee help just around the corner. Here are some places to start:

▼ The Small Business Association (SBA) (www.sba.gov) —Provides the small business owner with hands-on or on-line business and financing information including links to a number of government and non-governmental agencies.

▼ Small Business Development Centers (SBDC)—Provides managerial and technical help. Located on college and university campuses as well as through government funded and private business locations.

▼ Local college or university undergraduate and graduate students studying business and/or marketing

▼ SBA Business Information Centers (BIC)—Provides the tools needed for business plan development, product or service pricing, marketing and a host of other small business needs.

▼ The national or local Chamber of Commerce—Providing networking, marketing and mentoring opportunities (you can either join or pay a small fee to attend networking functions)

▼ Minority Business Development Centers (MBDC)

▼ The business reference section of your local library

▼ Trade associations and their publications

▼ American Demographics (www.demographics.com) for consumer market information

▼ The U.S. Federal Census Bureau (www.census.gov) for income, education, age and a considerable amount of information links pertaining to your target customer.

▼ The Department of Commerce's (www.doc.gov) Case Studies documentation where you'll find an enormous amount of useful regional statistical data to help you understand your target market.

▼ Dun & Bradstreet (www.dnb.com) or Dun & Bradstreet Small Business Services (www.sbs.dnb.com) for marketing services, supplier searches, women and minority owned business information, business credit ratings and more.

Some of these outlets will have enthusiastic people waiting to help you define your market and provide the building blocks for that important tool—your business plan.

## The Key to Success:

Always make sure that there is still a need for what you're offering and consider expanding your niche into new products or services.

*"It's simply a matter of doing what you do best and not worrying about what the other fellow is going to do."*
—John R. Amos

## Chapter 15
# Setting Yourself Apart

What is it that will set you apart from your competition? Is it something you offer that no one else has? Does your product or service have a patent or copyright so that the competition cannot legally copy it?

This is something that I can't tell you, but I can offer you some suggestions on how to discover those important and moneymaking differences.

If possible, sit down with a group of potential customers (whether they are family or friends) and ask them what's missing from their buying experience at their favorite store. For the sake of argument, let's create a fictitious retail outlet and call it Patrice's Party Store. Now let's ask some important questions: What's missing? Is it the customer service—no one's ever around when you have a question or maybe the staff isn't knowledgeable when it comes to a theme for a three-year-old's birthday party celebration. Could it be that Patrice's prices are higher than the large party superstores in the city, but they're willing to pay them anyway because Patrice is in the neighborhood—(she's convenient.) Are the employees rude and act as though they are doing you a favor instead of the other way around?

Not every one follows through with their good intentions—(you must know yourself, being a consumer of goods and services). There are firms that promise one thing and deliver something completely different. And fortunately for you, there will always be that menacing nuisance.

Why is that a good thing? Well, because you're a new business. And new businesses have a tremendous vantage point when it comes to delivering what the customer really wants and deserves. You can play upon the fact that your competition might have become careless in the customer service department and use it to your advantage by offering outstanding and sometimes uncommon service to your customers. For example: Most small business people stick to a prescribed set of working hours, i.e.: 9 a.m. to 5 p.m. which may not take into account the late hours potential customers may require because of commuting back and forth from their workplaces. For them, this leaves little time for taking care of personal necessities like making it to the dry cleaners before they close or the post office during the weekdays. What if you offered extended hours in the evening or began earlier in the day to accommodate your customers? It's something not every small business owner is willing or able to do.

## Self Check:

You may need to dig deeper into your target market to be certain that another level of uniqueness is justified and feasible before placing your product or service out there in the marketplace.

Over the years, I've noticed that people respond to what I call 'feel good' businesses. What do I mean by this? Well, as a consumer myself, I know that when I walk into a shop and purchase an item or service, I'm not only looking to buy a tangible or intangible thing, I want everything that goes with it; the shopping experience, a quality product or service and the assurance that if something does go wrong with it, I know that I can come back and get a replacement without feelings of 'return guilt.'

And as a small business owner, I've been told by my clients that they come back because they feel good about the experience and the product guarantee; so, I'm speaking from experience.

This is the kind of information you can use to stay ahead of the competition.

Another point to remember is that customers buy something because of what it can do for them and not because of what it is. This is something I learned in my first year as a corporate marketing representative for the IBM company. My colleagues and I referred to it as Marketing 101, basic knowledge!

Known as selling the benefits of a product or service instead of its features. When you practice it, this concept will always have your competition playing catch-up.

Here's an example of selling benefits over features: Let's pretend that you sell washing machines—

**The features are:**
1) Hot, cold and warm water settings
2) A programmable soak and rinse cycle
3) A volume control 'off' buzzer

**The benefits are:**
1) For clothes consisting of fibers and materials requiring different water temperatures to prevent shrinkage, excessive wrinkling and discoloration.

2) So you can have control over whether or when to add softener.

3) To enable users to locate the washer away from the living space— the buzzer will alert you when it's time to unload the clothes and place them in the dryer.

It would be a worthy exercise to write a half page or one page feature/benefit of your product or service so that when you're asked to describe what it is that you're selling, you don't just rattle off what it is—instead, you'll be able to add value to it by pointing out the benefits of your product or service to the consumer as well.

Features of my product or service:

_____

_____

_____

_____

Benefits of my product or service:

_____

_____

_____

_____

## The Key to Success:

Today, because of stiff competition, customer service should be in the forefront of every business owner's business thought process.

*"Becoming number one is easier than remaining number one."*
—Bill Bradley

## Chapter 16
# Branding

What is it and why is it important? Let's take a real life experience—yours. Look in your medicine cabinet at home or on your bathroom sink countertop. What kind of toothpaste or deodorant do you use? How long have you been using it? Would you consider switching? Why or why not? What about the make and model of the car you drive—the clothes you love to wear? How about the newspapers you read or the magazines you subscribe to or the foods you purchase at the supermarket? What about your telephone or Internet service? If you've found yourself always buying or subscribing to the same brand products year after year, then the company that manufactures and/or sells them has done an excellent job at branding.

### Self Check:
Here are a few things to consider when creating brand recognition for your enterprise:

▼ Look at the strengths of your business offerings and play them up

▼ Include exceptional quality, pleasant and positive service and a never-find-anywhere-else uniqueness

▼ Listen to what the buying public is saying about your product or service—through word of mouth or simple surveys

Let's take a look at the clothing you like to wear. Do any of the items in your closet have a company brand logo or label attached? Perhaps FUBU, Burberry, Phat Farm or DKNY? These examples are a sampling of businesses that purchase their retail apparel from outside manufacturers, attach their signature logos and/or label, then sells them to a retailer. Realistically, you could find the same or similar dresses, shirts or pants, minus the logo, in a lesser-known retail outlet at a lower price. But because of the recognizable tag and the brand it stands behind, consumers are willing and ready to dish out the extra cash.

Always make sure that your company name is synonymous with each product or service you introduce to the public. For example, when you see the Burger King logo, you automatically associate it with flame broiled taste, not fried.

You always want the consumer to associate your company with a positive experience and the highest quality product or service. The ability to create a loyal customer base or following for your product or service is what you should strive for.

Now this can be accomplished either using slick advertising campaigns or from the fact that your business has established itself as the expert in its field within and outside of its community borders.

Either way, 'brand loyalty' is a reachable goal—but it will take determination and a convincingly strong belief in your product or service to be able to attain it.

Don't be discouraged by the fact that older, more established businesses might have a greater share of a particular market. In fact, let that empower you to take a look at what the competition is providing, then add a little twist. Keep your eyes and ears open for opportunity, then firmly establish your niche! You know—niches don't always come knocking on your door. You might just have to go out and discover them.

## The Key to Success:

Simply put, 'branding' is the recognizable image of your company. It's what your firm stands for: quality, service, reliability, longevity and fun. Your products or services sell because of your business' characteristics.

*"Hire the best. Pay them fairly. Communicate frequently.
Provide challenges and rewards. Believe in them.
Get out of their way and they'll knock your socks off."*
—Mary Ann Allison

## Chapter 17
# The Price is Right

Have you ever wondered how a small business owner comes up with pricing for the products or services he or she is selling? There is a method to their madness and its simplicity or complexity is sometimes based on trial and error. Bear in mind that if your goods or services aren't priced right—there might not be any customers.

You may be under the popular assumption that small business owners decide by themselves alone what price to attach to their products or services. Wrong! Customers are really the ones who determine price. How? Because they either see your product or service as valuable or not.

How do you find out what price is acceptable? Get out there and talk to your potential customers and find out if what you intend to charge is on target, too high, or too low. Utilize the information from your market research data, i.e.: demographics, income, spending habits, etc., to gather relevant information to help determine what is or isn't acceptable.

As a consumer, you know all too well that before you shell out your hard earned cash to make a purchase, there are several factors that you take into consideration: the overall quality of the product or service, the perceived benefit to your lifestyle, the product or service's uniqueness, and its availability—and you do all of this in just a matter of seconds—subconsciously.

Now that the shoe is on the other foot, there are several factors that you'll have to consider before offering that product or service for sale. Take a look at what it cost to produce your product (including materials, labor, overhead), then determine what your desired profit margin (a percentage of the selling price) should be—keeping in mind what the market will bear and the lowest number you can go and still realize a profit.

It's also a good idea to know how much your competitors charge for products and services similar to what you're selling and then adjust your prices accordingly, whether up or down, depending upon the difference in value.

Always remain flexible in your pricing structure because of the nature and fickleness of the market.

Keep in mind that, just because you're the new kid on the block, it doesn't necessarily mean that you have to give away the entire farm! There is value in what you have to offer—never forget that. Your job is to make your product or service easily available to the buying public so that they can not only see and appreciate that value but are willing to pay a fair price to get it.

At most, pricing is a topic that can become very complicated and there are many books that will offer one formula or another for various pricing structures. Don't get bogged down with the fine points. If you've researched your industry, tested your target market and taken into account your overhead costs—you'll be okay. Just remember, if you need to re-adjust and tweak—just do it—the big guys do it all the time to keep the customers walking through their doors.

## The Key to Success:

The key point to remember here is that accurate pricing is crucial to the survival of your business.

*"When the doors of opportunity swing open,
we must make sure that we are not too drunk
or too indifferent to walk through."*
—Jesse Jackson

## Chapter 18
# Networking the Room

Some people have a natural flair for it; others have to muster up the courage to even consider doing it. However, networking is a fact of life for the entrepreneur—it's something you have to do if you want your venture to thrive.

Don't be overly concerned if you're not a social butterfly or the best conversationalist—all you really need to remember is that networking is the 'necessary means to a rewarding end.' That end could be in the form of collecting business cards at a networking event from potential clients, making a sincere effort to follow up in a day or two to continue a mutually beneficial conversation. Another end might be to meet one, two or even ten people who could either turn out to be your customers or introduce you to others who might need your services in the near future.

Even when you're in conversation with a person who's going on forever about nothing of importance, that 'idle chatter' could eventually lead to new business—it just might take an ounce more patience on your part.

Don't dismiss your family, friends and acquaintances as people you should 'press the flesh' with on a business level. If they hadn't thought of investing in your company or becoming a buying customer instead of just cheering you on before—maybe they'll reconsider after hearing your marketing pitch.

Take a couple of minutes and write down a few ideas on how you might approach networking, and remember, there's not an art to it. For most of us, it merely requires some pre-planning.

_____

_____

_____

_____

_____

Now that you have decided on how you want to approach networking, you'll need to find actual places to network in. First look to industry trade groups, organizations and your local Chamber of Commerce who sponsor "mixers" for their members and new business owners who are considering membership. These events encourage an 'exchange' atmosphere. But it won't happen by magic. If you're shy, force yourself to walk up to someone you don't know and just say 'hello.' They should respond with a greeting and then it's all up for grabs! Either you or your new potential client can begin the smooooooth transition to 'business talk.' Describe what you do, ask what they do—a few minutes of give and take. That's all there is to it...and it really does work.

But please don't forget the human aspect of business. You still need to put on that smiling face, polish off your positive attitude and release that friendly nature.

People do business with people they like. Here's a benefit to networking you may not have thought about—skills—finding a pool of talented business owners who could help you not only as customers but also if you're still in the market for an accountant or attorney. It's even possible that a banker could be the guest speaker at a networking event offering services you're not receiving at your present banking facility. Or he might be the one to help get you that loan you'll need in the future—prompting you to switch banks before you'd evened considered it. The meetings and information you receive could turn out to be priceless!

Keep in mind that networking doesn't just occur in buildings. Whenever you leave your home-based or storefront business, you get the chance to schmooze.

> **Here are a few everyday examples of places to network:**
> ▼ At your son or daughter's sporting events or even your own
> ▼ At the gym
> ▼ When you're socializing after church
> ▼ At the beauty salon or barbershop
> ▼ On-line
> ▼ At family or friends social gatherings
> ▼ At the doctor's or dentist's office

Don't pass up the service organizations that meet on a regular basis: Urban League, NAACP, Links, National Coalition of 100 Black Women, 100 Black Men, National Council of Negro Women, Jack & Jill of America, church services and conventions, and fraternities and sororities whose chapters can be found in nearly every town or city. At times these organizations might be in need of a speaker with your expertise for an event—call 'em up and volunteer to do it—you never know who might be in the audience. If you do it right, word spreads quickly and before you know it, you'll get an invitation to speak for another group. All the while you're building up your customer list and following up on the most promising leads. And soon, because of your well-publicized knowledge and new contacts, you'll be able to turn those volunteer gigs into a paid service.

When it's all said and done, networking is really an inexpensive way to meet a lot of people while advertising your business. All you're really doing is asking for the opportunity to talk with other entrepreneurs and business owners about your passion and in turn listening to what they have to say about theirs. And in the course of conversation, you could be building a lasting and profitable business relationship.

## The Key to Success:

The key to effective networking is planning—mapping out what you want to accomplish—whether it's fine-tuning your one-minute pitch about your product or service or brushing up on your listening skills.

*"Thoughts have power; thoughts are energy. And you can make your world or break it by your own thinking."*
—Susan Taylor

## Chapter 19
# What Are You Gonna Name It?

Naming your business is just as important as what you're offering for sale. The name of your business creates a lasting image in the eye of the consumer. But hold on for just a second before you pull out 'Bubba's Book of Business Names.' You should know that if the firm will be called anything other than your own full legal name, you may be required by your municipality or state government to register that name as a DBA, (doing business as). To do that, you should contact your county clerk's office and file an application. Costs vary but typically range between $10 and $100.

In some states you may be required to run an ad in the local newspaper to make sure the name you've chosen is not already taken. The length of time you run the ad varies, but in most states it must run in consecutive editions. There are some newspapers that will print your ad and file the necessary paperwork with the city or county for an additional fee, saving you much needed time. Don't forget to inquire.

The DBA, also known as a fictitious business name will be needed when you open a business bank account. And in some cities, towns or states the bank will need to see the actual fictitious name certificate—so don't get caught short. Always be prepared.

There are no hard and fast rules as to naming your venture, and quite frankly, a lot of debate goes on in prestigious business schools and expensive marketing firms as to what makes one name work and another one fail. Think about this—how many business names have you run across that seemed to have nothing to do with the product they're selling? For example, Kinko's (the copy store) is a coined name that works, is recognizable and is a successful venture!

Some companies turn to marketing firms to come up with a winning name and some just go with instinct or with luck and a prayer. But if you choose to retain a firm, be prepared to shell out a few thousand to many thousands of dollars for them to come up with the perfect name for your business using research tools, experience as to what works and why, to finding out if a particular name has been registered and trade-marked with another business—keeping you out of legal hot water.

Having said all of that, you should still be asking, 'Can't I do it on my own?' And the answer to that question would be, 'You'd better believe you can!' And because most entrepreneurs and small business owners have limited funds, they do just that.

## Ask Yourself:

- ▼ What am I trying to communicate with the name?
- ▼ What kind of customers am I trying to attract?
- ▼ Who are the customers I'm trying to attract?
- ▼ Is it too ethnic?
- ▼ Does the name make good business sense?
- ▼ Does it have anything to do with what I'm selling?
- ▼ Am I'm choosing a name that my customers will easily remember?
- ▼ Is it too long?
- ▼ Too short?
- ▼ Too confusing?
- ▼ Do I like it?

Compile a list of potential names and try them out on friends and family—paying close attention to their initial reaction. Ask yourself if you're comfortable saying it out loud? Are others? First impressions tell us a lot in the business world.

Be careful not to box yourself in—consider your expansion plans when naming your firm. You wouldn't want to call your shop: Mama's Soup Kitchen when you plan on offering a full range of hot home cooked meals, plus a well-stocked salad bar in the future or Kyle's Fish and Tackle if your future plans include expanding into golf, basketball and soccer gear. Mama's Homestyle Cooking or Kyle's Sporting Goods Store might be more appropriate, although I'm sure you would be much more creative.

Once you've done the primary research and given the final five to ten names serious consideration, wait a week or two and try the names on for size again. Hopefully by now the list has gotten even shorter.

When dreaming up the business name, you should also take into consideration any signage you might need for your storefront and also how the name and logo will appear on the business cards, stationary and your advertising media.

Once you've made a decision on the top two names, it's time to check to make sure the number one choice isn't already taken. This is an extremely important step—researching the name, because once you've made your final decision, you wouldn't want to have dreamed up the perfect name, open the doors to your business and find out that another firm has been operating under the same name for years. Contact the Secretary of State's office and find out which jurisdiction 'name registration' falls under.

## FYI:

To protect yourself even further, you might also want to register that name through the U.S. Patent and Trademark Office (www.uspto.gov). Basically, what this does is serve notice to other firms that your business name is taken and cannot be used without permission and compensation.

You might want to call several trademark attorneys for a quote on having this search done for you—or even firms specializing in trade name research for comparison—this could get expensive, so gather reputable references from other business owners in the area if you choose to make use of these services. Is it absolutely necessary for all small firms to trademark their business name? Of course not. But if you want to protect the name you've so carefully chosen and the brand that it represents, then it's something that you should take into consideration.

## The Key to Success:

All in all this should be an exciting part of starting a business, so don't forget to have fun with your creativity.

*"The more successful we have become,
the more intense the competition."*
—Byron Lewis

## Chapter 20

# The Competition

Competition is just another fact of life. There is always something or someone right around the corner with a bigger, better or faster product than what you have to offer. But don't let that scare you. On the contrary—it should only serve to empower you—keep you thinking. Simply be aware that the next entrepreneur or established business is waiting to fill your shoes and take your share of the market. So what do you do to crush the competition?

▼ Find out everything you feel you need to know about what they're selling and why customers choose to spend their money with them

▼ Pick apart their strategies and the way they operate.

▼ Study their strengths and their weaknesses

▼ What is the image they're portraying to the public?

▼ What makes them attractive to their customer set?

▼ Once you discover their market appeal—ask yourself if you can you do it better or differently?

▼ Observe their customer service—a key factor in any business. Any flaws?

▼ Develop a superior measure of customer satisfaction.

How do you go about accomplishing all of this? Look to your industry for any developing or established consumer trends that your competition may have overlooked. Find out where the competition is and go to their shops—pretend you're a customer.

## Ask Yourself:

▼ Were the personnel knowledgeable?

▼ Was there quick and friendly service?

▼ What makes their business unique?

▼ What are they offering that makes a customer feel that they must get their product or service from him/her.

▼ How are they displaying similar products?

▼ What forms of advertising are being used? i.e.: newspapers, flyers, coupon mailers, radio or cable TV spots?

▼ What is their pricing structure? i.e.: mark-up percentage (based on your knowledge of a particular product or service)

▼ Was the product selection adequate? Or were the shelves nearly bare?

Visit the stores at different days and times of the week and track the customer traffic flow.

▼ Observe the customers.

▼ What are they buying and how much?

▼ What are they saying about their buying experience?

▼ Are they concerned with the price of the product or service?

Don't be afraid to ask them why they shop there.

Become a customer and buy a product from your competitor.

▼ What was the quality of the product?

▼ Was the shop neat or messy?

▼ Was the location of the shop convenient?

▼ Would you shop there again? If so, why—if not, why not?

Call a competitor and pretend to be a potential supplier or vendor (You can be certain they have already done or will do the same to you). Find out what his policies and terms are relating to:

▼ payment terms for goods/products sold
▼ product discounts
▼ shipment or delivery schedules
▼ guarantees/warranties

Rate your overall experience as a shopper, buyer, supplier or vendor.

**Utilize technology**—use the Internet to get useful information about the competition. Go to the chamber of commerce and ask for general company materials and information. The business reference section of your local library has an extraordinary amount of information. Your reference librarian will be helpful in pointing you in the right direction. There you'll find books containing specific industry statistics, trade journals, newspapers and newsletters. They'll also have data on customer buying patterns with forecasts of current and future market trends.

## FYI:

National and local industry associations can be found listed in various directories such as the Business Information Source. Demographic information can be found in publications like: American Demographics, (www.demographics.com), Statistical Abstract of the United States, (www.census.gov) and the Rand McNally Commercial Atlas and Marketing Guide.

The Thomas Register, (www.thomasregister.com) and the Thomas Regional (www.thomasregional.com) offer an on-line resource of companies and products manufactured in the U.S. and the Harris Industrial Directories contain information on size, assets and location of your competitors. The Dun & Bradstreet (www.dnb.com) Regional Business Directory discloses company financials and credit rating information. Valuable historical data, i.e.: when the company was started, number of employees, and sales numbers can also be found in the D&B volumes.

Once again, never underestimate the power of networking. Mingle with your competitors at trade shows—talk to them at their booths—find out what they're thinking or planning.

When thinking of ways to attack the competition, keep in mind that most large companies and firms that have been around for some time lack a crucial element of endurable success—flexibility. This is where you can excel. As an entrepreneur, you're not afraid to fiddle with 'perfection' if you find that a product or service isn't bringing in the dollars that you initially expected it would. Larger firms may not be willing to set aside any more funds to an already established product or service and smaller firms may not be sharp enough to do so.

In this chapter we touched on just a few ways to discover how your competitor might be conducting business—there are plenty more. Some of which you'll find out after utilizing my suggestions; others you'll determine on your own—and all of which can help you stay ahead of the game.

## The Key to Success:

Remember, you're on a mission to fulfill your entrepreneurial dreams and goals, and answers and foresight are all that stands between success and failure.

*"The measure of a man's success must be according to his ability. The advancement he makes from the station in which he was born gives the degree of his success."*
—Sir Walter Besant

## Chapter 21
# One Size Doesn't Fit All

Way back in the beginning of the guide we discussed the different business structures you'll have to choose from. In this chapter we'll explore them in greater detail.

## Sole Proprietorship

This is a business structure whereby you are responsible for all aspects of the business, including profits and losses. It is the simplest business formation and the least expensive—all that is normally required is a business license.

However, as a sole proprietor, you are personally responsible for your company's liability—meaning your personal assets (home, car, bank accounts), are all at risk for seizure should there be any legal claims filed against the business.

Still yet, many entrepreneurs operate as sole proprietorships because of the ease in getting started and the total control they stand to enjoy.

Keeping in mind that raising start-up capital will likely come from your own savings or perhaps drawing from the equity in your home, this might also be a good time to ask for help from family and friends.

As we discussed earlier, banks and other lending institutions may be somewhat reluctant to wholly finance a sole proprietorship operation. So while there are many benefits to this business structure, there are also obstacles.

## Partnership

A Partnership is a business owned and operated by two or more people who share in the profits and losses of the firm (and not necessarily equally). Partnerships come in a couple of flavors—general and limited.

In a general partnership, each partner is liable for the debts of the enterprise. A limited partnership is just what it suggests—limited liability for the limited partner(s).

While the general partner(s) usually own and operate the business and take on unlimited liability, the limited partner(s) serve as investors whose liability is limited to the amount of their investment.

If you are structuring your business as a partnership, you must have a partnership agreement. No, it's not a legal requirement—but it would be foolish not to have it done.

Take for example a couple of guys who've enjoyed a friendship for over ten years and decide to go into business together. Who else would make better partners? They know each other's strengths and weaknesses and they've been known to finish each other's sentences when engaged in conversation. Even their wives and kids get along as if they're related. Sounds like those two are poster boys for success...NOT!

Forming a business partnership can be stressful for anyone—but for a couple of old buddies—you stand to lose more than the partnership if things don't go as planned—you could forfeit ten years of valuable memories and forever change the lives of two families. Don't chance it.

## The Partnership Agreement

Have an attorney draw up an agreement that's satisfactory for both parties. He or she will know what legalese to put into the document, but it will be up to you and your partner to answer these types of questions:

▼ What will each partner contribute to the partnership, i.e.: capital, equipment, etc.

▼ What will the responsibilities of each partner be?

▼ How long do you expect the partnership to last?

▼ How will conflicts be resolved?

▼ What happens if one of the partners wants out?

▼ What happens if a partner dies?

Of course the agreement will be more extensive than what I've laid out—however, these questions give you an idea of what you should consider before taking on a partnership between friends, family or acquaintances.

## Corporations

The Corporation (also known as a 'C' corporation) is a legal entity in the eyes of the law, separate from the people who formed it. And as such, the corporation has rights and privileges including the ability to raise capital by selling stock, borrow money and buy and sell real estate.

The liabilities of a corporation are separate from those of its shareholders, making it a more attractive business structure. But the costs are greatly higher than those of a sole proprietorship or a partnership.

The rules and regulations of chartering or registering a corporation differ from state to state and are subject to more government regulations than the other business structures. They are more complex to set up and require extensive accounting measures. I would strongly suggest consulting an attorney for this structure.

Benefits of a corporation are the limited liability protection it provides its owners (your personal assets are never considered when settling a debt) and the life of the corporation is not dependent on the life of its shareholders.

Drawbacks of owning a corporation include double taxation. Income earned by the corporation is subject to both federal and state taxes and any earnings distributed to shareholders as dividends are taxed once more on their individual tax returns.

The S Corporation (or Subchapter 'S' corporation) has the liability protection of a 'C' corporation, with a noticeable added benefit—no double taxation. Like a general partnership, income and losses are passed through the corporation to the shareholder's personal income tax return, up to the amount that person has invested, however, the number of shareholders is limited to seventy-five.

## Limited Liability Company or (LLC)

The Limited Liability Company or (LLC) combines the best qualities of a partnership (pass-through earnings and losses) and a corporation (limited liability protection.) The LLC operates as a legal entity as does a corporation, but unlike the 'S' corporation, is not limited to seventy-five shareholders. The disadvantages of an LLC, like a corporation, is cost. It can be expensive to form this type of business structure and in some states the death of an owner could end the LLC. I've drawn a comparison chart in Appendix A of the business structures to give you a side by side view of the advantages and disadvantages so that you can easily glance at what each one entails. This should provide additional help when you are considering how to set up your business.

## The Key to Success:

There are several types of business structures…choose carefully.

*"A young person, to achieve, must first get out of his mind
any notion either of the ease or rapidity of success.
Nothing ever just happens in this world."*
—Edward William Bok

## Chapter 22
# What's in your Plan?

Your business plan will be your map or guide to achieving the goals you established way back in Chapter 2. With this map, you'll be able to test-drive your business concept.

And when it's time to seek outside financing for your venture, the first document any investor or lender will want to see is your business plan. The plan will give you a clearer picture of how much capital will be needed for a successful business launch and estimate your financial requirements in the future. So take your time—it's not a document you can put together in a week or month.

## The Mission Statement

Remember when we talked about having a vision way back in Chapter 1. Well, the Mission Statement further illustrates that vision. The Mission Statement defines your business goals and objectives. It provides answers to the questions: What products will I offer? What service will I provide? What market will I target? At what rate will I grow?

The mission statement is all about action. It doesn't have to be long or complicated—it only has to be meaningful, measurable and achievable.

**Self-Check:**

To put it all in perspective, a business plan should include:

❏ Mission Statement
❏ Executive Summary
❏ Business Concept
❏ Market Strategies
❏ Competitive Analysis

❏ Organizational and Operational Plan
❏ Financial Analysis
❏ Growth Forecasts

## Executive Summary

A one page digestible description of the business and it must have an instant impact on the reader (banker, investor) to entice him or her to read on. It should clearly state the nature of the business—service, retail, distribution or manufacturing and your target market. Also included in the executive summary is the business structure and the management team.

Although the Executive Summary appears first in your plan—it should be written last—why? Because after everything else is written, you'll have a better picture and feel for every aspect of your venture right in front of your eyes—in black and white.

## Business Description

An expanded executive summary detailing your products or services, who you are targeting and why there is a need for outside financing. It outlines the industry and describes its growth trends. It describes your distribution methods and your approach to customer service. This is your chance to brag about the unique qualities of your product or service, promotional game plans and expected revenues.

## Market Research

A description of the industry and your niche in it. It should describe the nature of your market, i.e.: trends, size, sales and growth potential. The market research section should tell who your customer is, where they're located, why and when they will buy your product or service and projected sales numbers based on that information.

Market data should demonstrate your share of the market, reveal how you plan to capture it and make clear how your company will stand out from the rest in the industry.

## Competitive Analysis

An expanded version of how you will stand apart from the competition. What is your competitive advantage? Is it that you have a newer or better product to offer to the customer? Is your customer service second to none? What are your competitor's weaknesses—their strengths and how will your firm function to keep new competition at a minimum? What strategies will you have in place to ward off the competition? All of these questions need to be answered in the competitive analysis section of the business plan. You'll be able to make use of information gathered from other sections of the plan to assist in the research.

## Organizational and Operational Plan

Description of your management team and their role in the day to day operation of the business. A listing of each manager's biographical skills, education and qualification and how it benefits the venture is described here. The day-to-day function of the business is described in this section as well as the legal structure you've chosen for your firm. (if you're operating as a sole proprietorship, the organizational structure will only reflect your role.)

## Financial Analysis

A financial forecast of your business. It shows long and short-term profitability. From the financial analysis come the income statement, cash flow statements and the balance sheet. Because this section of the business plan requires a great deal of financial projections (because the business is not operational yet) I would suggest recruiting the help of your bookkeeper, accountant or an accounting software package to step you through it. Remember—if at any time you require outside financing for your venture, investors and other lending institutions will be most interested in the financial section of your business plan.

When requesting a loan, you should be specific as to the purpose, the dollar amount, time frame for repayment and the investors return on the investment.

## Growth Forecast

This is the fun section of the plan. You get to discuss how you intend to take a fledgling firm from the start-up phase to different stages of positive growth. This might entail introducing new products or services in order to bring in new customers or expansion plans to include e-commerce.

In Appendix C, I've listed some of the more popular software packages that can assist you when preparing your business plan.

Now I know I've just given you a lot of information to digest. This is probably a good time to get up, walk around and clear your head.

The key to remember is this: Don't try to take it in all at once and become so overwhelmed that you put the guide away, never to be read again. That would be a terrible mistake—and very unlike the entrepreneurial spirit that you have inside.

Simply take what you need—when you need it—then do it.

I've read business books that looked and read like encyclopedias—information overload! So, I learned to take small pieces of the pie, carefully chewing it then swallowing it slowly, savoring the lasting flavor—thoroughly enjoying the experience.

This is what I encourage you to do with this entrepreneurial guide—read small sections of the information that you need, when you're ready—understand the contents, apply it to your specific entrepreneurial idea and then execute it to the best of your ability when it comes time to launch.

### The Key to Success:
The road to success takes many unexpected turns, so you'll need a good map to keep you heading in the right direction.

*"A business that makes nothing but money
is a poor kind of business."*
—Henry Ford

# Chapter 23
# Show Me the Money!

You've already made the most important step in the business process—deciding to start. The next phase is how to finance the venture.

Now, because you're just getting started, banks and other lenders or investors may not likely come knocking on your door offering you large sums of money, in the beginning. So the best place to look is in the mirror.

Entrepreneurs and small business owners all over the country will tell you that the number one question banks, government lending resources and investors will want answered is how much of your own money you have invested in this idea. These people want to know how much faith you have in this unproven enterprise—what you've done and are willing to do to raise capital.

You must be wondering where on earth you are going to find enough seed money to even get started.

Let's begin by looking into your bank accounts, retirement accounts, home equity, or your car. You don't necessarily have to sell your home or car—using them as collateral for a loan might work best in your situation. What about the cash value in a life insurance policy?

Before you decide to borrow against your home, car, IRA or insurance policy, talk to a financial professional or read the fine print of those documents to make sure you don't get slapped with any withdrawal or late repayment penalties.

You might have to pull out those credit cards and take a cash advance to help finance your dream—Remember Robert Townsend, the comedian/actor and movie director who used his credit cards to finance his first film production, Hollywood Shuffle? Don't forget Spike Lee whose credit cards and grandmother came to his rescue in making the film, She's Gotta Have It in 1986—a film made for about $170,000 and grossed more than $7 million!

This is also the time to tap family and friends for additional capital. These are people who already know you and are willing to loan you a sum of money based on your character and integrity.

But don't just take the money and run. I suggest drawing up a loan agreement—nothing complicated—just an agreement stating who loaned you the money and for what purpose. Also included should be a start and end date for repayment.

There are times when borrowing money from family and friends can be somewhat unpleasant or even embarrassing. Some will want management control over the business in return for their investment, acting as if they are more qualified to run the venture than you are.

Others will loan you money with pressured warnings attached, such as: "If I loan you the money, you have to promise that I get at least a double return on my investment within six months to a year." While that may be possible, it's not something that you can definitely 'promise.' In the start-up phase, growth is based on forecasted projections of the market—not promises.

It's best to stay clear of friends or relatives who have ulterior motives. And certainly don't let your need for seed money back you into a financial corner. Understand the difference between being needy and being desperate.

Once you've retained real interest from a friend or relative, treat them professionally, as you would any other lender—(that's who they are for the purposes of your business meeting).

Always keep the personal relationships separate from any business discussions or transactions. Explain your business concept in detail, describing how their financing will be utilized.

You might want to work out a monthly or semi-monthly status report of the business if the lender/investor won't be directly involved in the day-to-day operations.

Remember, don't make anything more complicated than it needs to be. A simple half page or one page update on where the business stands at any given point in time should be sufficient. Lenders or investors want to be kept in the know, not aggravated by 'TMI' (too much information.) Just make sure he or she is in tune with your plan and excited about the business and its potential. Never under-estimate the power of enthusiasm!

Now if you decide to go to your community bank for capital resources, let me prepare you for some of the pre-qualification criteria they'll look for in a potential loan candidate.

## Did You Know?

Traditionally, bankers make their loan decisions based on the five C's:

▼ Character (of the small business owner)

▼ Capital (on hand and requested)

▼ Capacity (to repay the loan)

▼ Collateral (what you own that can be used as loan security)

▼ Credit (personal credit history past and present)

I've seen, interviewed and personally met with African American entrepreneurs who've been denied a loan or credit for no other reason than for the fact that they are African American entrepreneurs. In this day and age it's a sad reality. However, it is something that we've had to find creative ways around and there are plenty of us who are extremely inventive. The bank's reasons can be anything from 'I see you've had some credit issues in the form of a bankruptcy, overdue loans or credit card payments,' to 'your business plan is poorly written or missing critical financial information' or 'your firm has no track record.'

Of course these are problems that need to be addressed, but you know as well as I do that blacks aren't the only one's with blemishes on their credit reports. The question becomes: "Where can I go and sit down with someone who is willing to work with me on a business level today despite my personal financial hardships of the past?"

Such people do exist, but you'll have to be well prepared mentally and business-wise to overcome those financial hurdles before approaching them.

James Blanks, Vice President, Commercial Loan Manager of First Independence National in Detroit, Michigan suggests that any entrepreneur be ready to "Tell their story concisely, succinctly and factually." "Be prepared to discuss your financial needs, how you plan to market your business and repay your loan." Blanks goes on to say that past credit issues shouldn't prevent you from attempting to secure a loan or line of credit. "Every case is unique," he says. "Variables such as personal collateral and business cash flow are taken into consideration."

"Lack of preparation and lack of collateral are two areas where entrepreneurs and small business owners need to focus before approaching a banker," says Derek Grayson, Vice President, Commercial Banking Division of the Citizens Trust Bank of Atlanta. "I can't stress enough how important it is to have a business plan that spells out what the business is involved in and its projected financial statements. You really have to be able to articulate what's in that plan and how you came up with the information." For those businesses that don't have a track record, your personal credit history is crucial. Grayson points out that banks look at the last 24 months of how you've repaid your debt.

Some entrepreneurs and small business owners have turned to an increasingly popular method of financing known as factoring, (a process where financial institutions give you access to a credit line based on your company's account receivables and outstanding invoices.) Though this route may seem like an unfavorable alternative, sometimes we may have to take a detour before we can reach our final destination.

But, for now, let's say that the five C's pose no challenge for you whatsoever—you can now pass Go. What information will a lender want to know? As I mentioned, they'll definitely scrutinize your business plan and your financial statements. They'll want to know how much money you need to borrow and for what purpose that cash will be used. And, most important, how the loan will be paid back.

## FYI:

Here are some of the loan products available to small business owners:

**Line of credit**—short-term loan for a period of one year extending the cash available in your checking account for working capital, inventory and cyclical business needs.

**Installment loan**—funding for a variety of needs including real estate—cash available upon contract signing. Terms vary according to loan use.

**Secured loan**—available to new business owners who pledge acceptable collateral (defined by the lender)

Think carefully about your answers—bankers are a tough and sometimes intimidating crowd. (I strongly suggest before taking a trip to the bank, you visit a Small Business Development Center or meet with the folks at SCORE to go over your business plan in detail and to prep you on your business presentation. You always want to appear professional and be prepared. Don't give the banker any reasons to say no.)

There are large banks and small community banks. The ones most likely to hear your plea for capital are your neighborhood banking institutions. So get your papers in order, state your purpose for the loan and be prepared to pull out your full arsenal of credit worthiness. Give it all you've got and remember: the answer can either be an empowering yes or a disappointing no—but true entrepreneurs never give up.

Knowing that small businesses are the backbone of our country, (a view not lost on the federal government), there is an understanding that you, the entrepreneurs, are the people who create the most jobs—not the giant corporations.

And to that end, the government is willing to step in financially when others have turned you down—more than likely because you've failed to meet the five-C criteria. So, if you've been previously denied credit, you should ask the bank if they would reconsider making the loan if the SBA backed it.

The Small Business Administration offers SBA-guaranteed loans to new businesses that may not otherwise qualify under traditional criteria. The SBA itself does not make the loan—they guarantee participating banking institutions that if you fail to repay your business loan, they will payback a certain percentage (85%) of the loan.

The criteria for qualifying for an SBA backed loan, (equity, collateral) is less strict than what is required from commercial banking institutions. Lenders who participate in the SBA program are classified as regular, certified (those who have met certain criteria and have been involved heavily in SBA loan activity and are given partial lending authority) or preferred lenders (those who are considered SBA's most favored lenders and are given full lending authority.)

A list of the SBA's small business-friendly banks can be found on the SBA web-site under Financing Your Business and Small Business Lenders. Locate your state and find a lender in or near your community.

Although this seems like a win-win situation, and in a lot of cases it is; be prepared to have your personal credit history inspected and depending on the loan program, you could be subjected to filling out a stack of paperwork.

The initial process starts when the private lender accepts your application. The application is then sent to the SBA where it is then reviewed again and approved. The lender then disburses the funds to you, the borrower.

## FYI:

To find out even more about SBA loan offerings, visit their web-site at www.sba.gov or call the SBA Answer Desk at 1-800-8-ASK-SBA for information about how to get assistance in your area.

The SBA offers the following loan programs:

▼ **7(a) Loan Guaranty Program**—The SBA guarantees 75% of the total loan amount up to $750,000. For loans less than $150,000 the guarantee can be as much as 85%. Uses for this loan include but are not limited to expansion, inventory, equipment, working capital and real estate.

▼ **Low Doc**—A one-page application, with quick processing of two to three business days on loans up to $150,000. This program lives up to its name of low documentation. However, it does rely heavily upon your credit rating, personal character, your business experience and cash flow.

▼ **SBA Express**—This loan is similar to the Low Doc offering in speed and amount, up to $150,000. The SBA Express program authorizes its preferred lenders to use their own documentation and procedures to process and service an SBA backed loan without having to wait for SBA approval. Up to 50 percent of this type of loan is guaranteed, and loans under $25,000 require no collateral from the borrower.

▼ **7(m) Microloan Program**—Under this program, the SBA provides loans for entrepreneurs needing financing as low as $100 up to $35,000. Funding is made through nonprofit brokers who in turn make the loan available to entrepreneurs. The application process is fast, usually less than a week.

▼ **CAPlines**—the CAPline loan was designed to provide working capital for seasonal and cyclical business needs, i.e.: material costs for construction projects.

The CAPline can be used like a credit card with a revolving balance or a non-revolving line of credit paid over an established period of time. The SBA provides guarantees up to 85% on loans up to $750,000. There are five programs operating under the CAPline program:

1) Contract loan program—used for contract labor and material financing.

2) Seasonal line of credit—used to help finance a rise in accounts receivable, inventory and additional labor during peak seasons.

3) Small asset-based line—lines of credit up to $200,000 for use in inventory purchase, labor cost or financing accounts receivable.

4) Standard asset-based line—similar to the small-asset base line program, but with higher loan amounts—over $200,000 and stricter requirements.

5) Builder's line of credit—Provides financing for small general contractors involved in residential or commercial construction.

▼ And of course there is the **SBA 504 Loan Program**—providing long-term, fixed-rate financing for acquisition of capital assets like real estate and equipment.

The SBA 504 loans provide funds up to $1 million dollars and as you might expect, the loan process is different from its SBA cousins in that they are made through SBA Certified Development Companies (CDC) servicing communities throughout the country.

As a small business owner applying for a 504 loan in the million-dollar range, you'll be required to finance at least 10 percent of the borrowed amount while the bank and the CDC put up the remaining percentage.

▼ There is also the **SBA Pre-qualification Loan Program**—designed to help in the loan pre-qualification process for women and minorities. Loan amounts can reach up to $250,000. You will need to have your business plan prepared (the SBA can assist you).

An SBA chosen go-between submits the application along with your business plan to the SBA who issues a pre-qualification letter upon approval which you then take to the bank with your application package. Because of the SBA guarantee, you are more likely to receive a favorable reply from the lender.

▼ And no doubt you've heard of the **Minority Business Development 8(a) Program**—whereas a business, operational for at least two years and 51 percent minority owned by a socially or economically disadvantaged U.S. citizen (racial, ethnic, cultural, gender, disabled) be given access to lucrative government contracts, training and counseling.

These programs are widely known as set-asides. In order to qualify, participants must be certified as a Minority Business Enterprise (MBE) through the SBA.

Since 1996, the SBA has been guaranteeing loans for franchise ownership.

## The Key to Success:

If you're not willing to lay out the cash—why should anyone else risk their fortunes on your dream?

*"Leadership…can only be demonstrated through example…
I never ask someone to do something that I wouldn't do
or haven't done.*
—Emma Chappell

# Chapter 24
# I.O.U.

As a new enterprise, you'll want to establish a credit policy for your customers. Aside from the convenience it provides to your market, it can also improve your cash flow.

Research has shown that companies who accept credit cards benefit from an increase in customer spending. Shoppers will use credit cards to make large purchases when they don't have the ready cash on hand or their checkbooks available. Even if they hadn't planned on buying at all, there's a greater chance that they'll make an impulse buy where credit cards are accepted.

Cash flow is improved because of the promise of payment that comes with credit card guarantees and use of those funds in a matter of days. While credit cards pose less of a threat in receiving payment for merchandise sold or services performed, it's not as easy as calling up a bank and requesting a credit card merchant account.

You'll need to do your homework when it comes time to choosing a bank that'll grant you merchant status for MasterCard and Visa.

American Express and Discover issue their cards directly. Talk to other business owners for bank recommendations. And as always, ask questions—find out if they're satisfied with the services they receive.

Expect to pay a number of fees for the privilege and convenience of accepting credit cards including a transaction fee each time a customer makes a purchase. But like anything else in business, you'll have to weigh the risks and go with what you feel is right. Eventually, as your enterprise grows, market demands may help to influence your final decision.

Today, it's not unusual to see consumers using debit cards as their card of choice for making purchases. The difference between a credit card and a debit card is self-explanatory. A credit card grants the customer extended credit for a set amount of time. With a debit card, the money is immediately debited from the customer's checking account. There are no checks to write and no future bills or invoices. The benefit to you is that a debit card gives you immediate access to the cash. Check with your financial institution regarding fees associated with setting up debit card transaction capability.

Making the decision to accept checks can be a sticky one. There's bound to be a customer who will bounce a check due to insufficient funds in his or her account or the client who issues a stop payment order after receiving your product or service. These are some of the realities of conducting business and there'll be times when you can stop it ahead of time by taking certain precautions but there might be instances where it becomes necessary to recoup the funds through the courts.

Thousands of businesses use check verification and guarantee services like TeleCheck for quick check approval. The charge for this service is minimal compared to the peace of mind you have when accepting checks from customers. And their guarantee policy states that you will be refunded the full value of a check that was initially approved but later turns out to be no good.

## The Key to Success:

Because you're a start-up, most banks will look at your personal tax returns and the profitability of the company before issuing merchant status. Others will look at that, plus how long you've been in operation.

*"The very first law in advertising is to avoid
the concrete promise and cultivate the delightfully vague."*
—Bill Cosby

# Chapter 25
# Advertising

The 'lifeblood' of your business depends on advertising. This is the way to target specific customers who'll want to buy your product or service.

Once you understand where your customers are and what interests them—their hobbies, age, likes and dislikes and how much disposable income they have, (money they use to buy good and services) you'll begin to understand which advertising medium you should be using.

For most entrepreneurs and small business owners, print media is the least expensive way to go initially as opposed to broadcast. Newspapers are an excellent way of spreading the word of a new business in town—for free!

Editors and reporters are always looking for news. Call your local or statewide paper and tell them about your new and exciting venture. Pump it up! Convince them that what you have to offer is the best product or service ever to hit the market since hip-hop designer clothing or restaurant food delivery. You'd be surprised at the response and interest you'll get from such an article.

I've done it a few times…and it really does work. But you have to build the excitement by your spoken or written words. Ask the reporter or editor, once you sense an interest, if you should write the background history of the product—(you'll want to appear helpful.)

Remember, this is free advertising and something that will become part of your sales and promotional kit. Don't stop at one newspaper if they refuse to take you up on the offer. Try all of them—large, medium and small.

If you do choose the newspaper medium for advertising, find out if the editor has plans for an upcoming 'special features' section. I'm sure you've seen notices in the paper advertising a Technology issue or a New Homes or Bridal issue. If your business can cater to any of these industries or others in any way, shape or form, you'll definitely want to advertise in that issue—and in that section. Your target audience can't help but see you if you're there.

Now some entrepreneurs and small business owners will think you've totally lost it if you tell them you're placing an ad in a magazine. Their first thought would probably be "You'll never be able to afford it." But then you can look them dead in the eyes and say, "I've already done it—and at very little cost!"

'How is this possible?'—should be your next question for me. And I'd tell you that by picking up the phone and calling the publication you have an interest in advertising and asking if they have remnant space available—leftover space that has to be filled before going to print. Generally that space will be sold at discounted rates.

## Caution:

Magazine advertising may seem like a glamorous way of getting your product or service into the marketplace, but always keep your target customer in mind before making any commitment to advertising and determine if that in fact, is the best way to reach your desired audience.

A form of advertising that potential customers like to be able to take with them is the brochure. Granted, they may not have a lot of time to read through all the points and details of your business at the time they receive it—but if the brochure is well designed and the important information has been strategically placed—they'll get what they need up front, in order to make a buying decision.

Like all forms of advertising, the brochure should be exciting, not wordy. It should motivate the customer to take action—give them what they need and not a sentence more. You don't want them to put it down before understanding what you have to offer and the benefit they'll receive from having bought it.

Remember, your brochure is a tool to arouse interest and firmly plant the image of your business into the brain of your target market. Whether you decide to design and print it yourself or have it done by a graphic artist and printer—the aim should be to produce a professional looking document that would move the reader to buy the product or use the service.

Another cost effective way to advertise is direct marketing—coupons or direct mail. I'm sure you've received hundreds of coupons in the mail over the years, and other forms of advertising like brochures, letters, fliers and postcards. They've all found their way to your mailbox.

Think about what you do when you get them. I know—your first instinct is to get rid of them—throw them out. But wasn't there a time when you thumbed through the coupon mailers or read over a brochure or even taken the time to glide through a colorful flier or a scenic postcard? If you said yes to any of those scenarios—then the sender has benefited from a captive audience!

It may take a few repeat mailings to secure the actual sale, but the bottom line is that you'll have a customer. A shrewd way that I've seen coupons being used is on the Internet. As potential customers browse your Web-site, a coupon listing a discount for first-time users of your product or service is also displayed.

Have you ever come home and found a flier stuck in your door or tucked alongside the red flag on your mailbox? How about in the lobby of your apartment building? And how many times have you returned to your car on a parking lot and found one lying under your windshield wiper? C'mon, admit it—don't you take a quick peek before trashing it? If it's a restaurant flier, you might be willing to keep it for those times when it's too hot to cook or you're simply too tired. Once again, the sender has been effective in either making the sale now or in the near future.

## Ask Yourself:

▼ Have I targeted the right customer in my advertising campaign?

▼ What image am I communicating with my choice in advertising?

▼ Am I willing to set aside money for my advertising budget?

▼ Am I in a position to be able to give away my product or service now in order to receive benefits later?

▼ Will my business survive if I choose not to advertise right away?

Now I know we're in the 21st century, the age of technology when at the stroke of a key or through voice activation you can find almost anything on the Internet. But there are still quite a bit of us who still want to flip through those thin 'Yellow Pages' commonly referred to as 'the book' to find the telephone number or the address of a business that will service our needs at any given time.

Besides convenience, most people have found reliable answers to their business and personal questions neatly categorized throughout the pages of the book, which is more than reason enough to keep it around, sometimes on top of the refrigerator, or in a kitchen drawer or balancing a wobbly table or chair. And there are those of us who are guilty of holding onto the bulky book for years and years! But when it comes right down to it, everyone who has a phone—has had 'the book' delivered to his or her doorstep.

Advertising on the Internet has been a clever way to reach an audience without boundaries. However, the question to keep in mind is if you'd be reaching your intended customer. Today, most business owners have a Web-site to support their marketing, advertising and sales efforts. The cost is relative to the look and feel of the site—the design, monthly hosting, updating and maintenance. Or, if you're familiar enough with computer and Internet technology, you can do it itself.

It'll take some creativity on your part to get customers to visit your site: your business cards and company stationary should always include the Uniform Resource Locator (URL—the location of an electronic address). And on every ad you place, brochure you design and sample product you give away—the Web-site address should be clearly listed.

Once customers visit your site, you'll want to make sure that the content draws them back time after time.

All it takes is a 'clever hook' to get anyone's attention—and it really doesn't matter if it appears online or in 'the book.' The desired end result is a new customer for your product or service.

Although classified ads may not 'pack the house,' they can still be an effective and economical way to get your name out to the buying public. The key to classified advertising is to come up with a headline that catches the reader's attention.

For example: Look Younger in Minutes—to capture the attention of a target market of aging men and women. You can even use a similar approach for your 'Yellow Pages' ad—a strong headline with a different spin on it to make yours stand out from the other advertisers who are selling a similar product. Or simply using color in your yellow pages ad will draw more attention than plain black ink—(keep in mind that the cost may be more than what you're willing to pay initially.)

Call your local cable and radio stations for advertising costs. Ask about lower rates, i.e.: late night or early mornings. If the cost exceeds

113

your budget, don't give up too quickly. Find out if the station would be willing to give you free time in exchange for providing your product or service free of charge. As an entrepreneur, you have to come up with creative measures to get what you need and want.

Tips on measuring what works in advertising:

▼ When customers come into your shop or office, ask how they heard about your business

▼ If you offer discount coupons for first-time or returning customers, note the number of coupon returns or place a number sequence on the coupons for the various newspapers you might advertise in to see which paper(s) bring in the most customers

▼ When you place an ad for a particular product, take notice of its sales results

▼ If you've advertised a service—leave the customer wanting to find out more by calling your business number—then measure the numbers of calls wanting follow-up information.

## The Key to Success:

Advertising results take time. Be patient and make a commitment to stick with what works for your unique venture.

*"Imagine what a harmonious world it could be
if every single person, both young and old shared
a little of what he is good at doing."*
—Quincy Jones

## Chapter 26
# Publicity

Celebrity public relations (PR) firms are not the only companies who can send out press releases announcing to the world what their clients are involved in.

Large and small companies send out press releases every day to accomplish that very goal. It's a shrewd means of getting the word out about who you are, what your company is doing, why it's doing it, where it's happening and how the public can get in on it. And all of it can be carried out through the media and other mediums at virtually no cost to you!

And who better to shout about your firm…than you!

All of this can be accomplished by contacting your local television, radio, cable station or newspaper and announcing your expertise in a particular field—urging the media to contact your firm as the expert whenever there is a related 'forum for discussion' or if they happen to want to profile someone in your field of expertise, or if they need to call on someone with your skills to write an article for their publication.

You gain instant credibility as a solid business in the community with tremendous possibilities.

Maybe products similar to yours are the hot topic of the day or week. Jump on the 'vogue bandwagon.' Send samples along with company and contact information to the media outlet that's of interest to your target market.

## If there's no buzz...create it!

Contact newspaper editors or radio and television station programmers and suggest how your product or service would be an interesting topic for their readers or listening and viewing audiences.

I did it in 1986 when I designed and developed the Catch-It bib for new moms and dads whose clothing more often than not became the target of a well-fed infant's meal after a 'spirited burp.'

In the beginning, I started with a local marketing campaign, placing the bibs in specialty stores and boutiques, participating in church bazaars and through word of mouth, all of which brought in slow sales on a good day!

I knew I had to redirect my thinking and try for free advertising on a wider scale.

I picked a medium that I counted on every day for information and relaxation—the radio. I called a station in New York that had a weekly small business segment that reached the Tri-state area of New York, New Jersey and Connecticut.

I told them I'd created a wonderful and unique product no one else had and that I thought it would be perfect for a 'new and unusual product segment.' They bought the idea and I rushed into the city and took over a sample.

When the segment aired, more than fifty people called in, wanting to know how they could purchase the Catch-It bib! Not only was that a wonderful marketing experience...it was free advertising!

After that, I decided that mail order would deliver a more profitable venue for the bib than placing it in local specialty stores and I used the radio whenever I could do so at no cost and newspaper advertising coupled with magazine remnant space to promote and sell my product.

If opportunities similar to what I've just described presents itself to you—grab it! It could mean a significant difference in your marketing war chest!

After you send out press releases, volunteer to speak at business luncheons, organization meetings, and trade group conferences, always be prepared to hand out your company press kit.

## Did You Know?

A press kit should contain information about your firm:

▼ A short cover letter of introduction

▼ Product or service description and documentation

▼ Past articles written about the firm and its offerings

▼ A business card or two

▼ A brief bio about yourself

▼ A glossy photo can be included if you can afford the extra cost.

What's that you say? The fear of speaking to a group of strangers makes you break out in hives? Then what I'd suggest is that you start off by taking tiny steps…speaking to a small group, maybe three or four people about your business at a networking function or at a social or family gathering, slowly increasing that number at different venues.

## The Key to Success:

The key point to remember is that you are the expert at that moment—always be prepared to intelligently discuss your product or service, because once you have a captive audience, a new customer is not far behind.

*"When two men in business always agree,*
*one of them is unnecessary."*
—William Wrigley, Jr.

## Chapter 27
# Who You Gonna Call...?

As in...hiring people to help you achieve your business goals? You may not need to hire someone full-time—just part-time—maybe to help you during your busy season. Or it could be that you plan on running a consulting firm and you need specific skills to meet a customer's needs. In that instance, you might want to hire an independent contractor for that one particular job assignment.

But as an entrepreneur and new business owner, you might not want to take on too much too soon. The hiring of even one employee means establishing or adding on new business procedures. There's the interviewing process, the legalities, work standards you've instituted so far—even training. You have to take into consideration such things as vacation time and pay, sick days and pay, insurance and medical benefits.

Now, I'm not trying to discourage you from hiring employees in the beginning stages—I merely want to point out the options that you have available to you.

Whatever hiring decision you make, be sure to always write down the job you need that person to accomplish—whether short-term or long-term.

## Temporary Help

Today temporary employment agencies provide skills from secretarial to technology and everything in between. It used to be that companies would only go to temp agencies when their administrative staff called in sick. Now those same firms offer specialized skills from a competitive pool of workers, some of whom have been laid off from their jobs and others who've chosen to work on a temporary basis.

The agencies have already located, interviewed, prescreened and in some cases trained the applicants for you. So all you have to do is call—express your needs and wait for the individual to show up at your door. Of course before you do any of that, you'll want to know the reputation of the firm your dealing with. Talk to other small businesses that have used them—are they reliable—professional?

## Self Check:

Once you've made a decision to go with a particular firm—call 'em up and ask some questions:

▼ Discuss the fees for such services

▼ Find out if the firm is a member of the National Association of Temporary Staffing (NATS) www.natss.org. Why or why not?

▼ Inquire whether or not, they specialize in a particular skill set

▼ What happens if the temp doesn't work out—will they provide a replacement?

▼ Can they fill your staffing needs immediately?

▼ Do they provide liability insurance and workers' compensation for the temporary worker?

▼ Are there provisions for your firm to permanently hire the temporary worker if you decided to do so?

## Part-Time Help

Another option is to hire a part-timer. There are plenty of experienced, professional, retired folks looking to get back into the job market on a part-time basis for any number of reasons. For some, the glamour of retirement has yet to live up to all its promises, while for others, the extra money can be used to supplement their fixed income. This pool of workers could realistically provide you and your business with instantaneous knowledge that would otherwise take years to master on your own.

A relatively new source of finding qualified help is through a Professional Employer Organization (PEO). These companies handle the human resource (HR) responsibilities for small and large firms. Not only do they provide the staff, the PEO will take care of employment labor laws, payroll, insurance, and other HR related tasks allowing you to spend more time concentrating on your core business and fewer headaches from HR concerns. The employee works for the PEO, so income and employment taxes are paid by the PEO. Your company would pay a fee, a percentage of the gross wages (usually between 3 and 6 percent) according to your employee needs, i.e.: professional, managerial, administrative, etc., and how many workers you'd require. Although you may not be at this stage of the game quite yet—you should know that such companies exist to help lift the burden of business ownership and employee responsibilities.

### FYI:

To get more information on PEO's, contact the National Association of Professional Employer Organizations, www.napeo.org.

Don't shy away from the stay-at-home moms or dads! They may have decided to stay home with the kids but you'll find years of valuable experience and marketable skills among this group. And there might come a point in time when they're willing to market those skills again, part-time.

Not all high school students want to work in the fast food industry. Some have expert secretarial skills, which in today's environment, means personal computer literate and software savvy. Some students are competent in sports or talented musicians—others are lovers of the written word or technology guru's. Depending on the type of business you have, and the skills needed, you could very well find the perfect candidate in the 18 and under crowd. Check with high school counselors in your area for rules and regulations relating to the hiring practices of minors.

College students are always on the lookout for an opportunity to add 'real world' experience on their developing resumes. Try spreading the word around or placing a simple ad in the local classifieds or the school newspaper. Better yet, place a call to the career placement center at a college or university. In most cases you'll need to complete an application with your company's information and a job description so that the right candidates can respond to your request. You could be pleasantly surprised to find work-for-college-credit programs or internships already in place.

So as you can see, there are feasible options for cash strapped entrepreneurs—and it doesn't mean having to accept second best.

## The Key to Success:

Always write down the job description before hiring anyone. It can be used as a measuring tool if you hire a temporary employee, the foundation for a contract when using independent contractors or a job description for a permanent employee.

*"There are no secrets to success. It is the result of preparation, hard work, learning from failure."*
—Colin Powell

## Chapter 28
# Mentors

Teacher, trainer, coach, counselor, guru—you get the idea. A mentor is someone who is there for you when you need advice or a person who has offered you guidance on your trip down the sometimes, bumpy road to entrepreneurship and who won't abandon you once you arrive. That individual can be found in friends, former colleagues, associates, business partners, family…anyone who believes in you and your dream.

You may not even have had the good fortune of meeting your mentor yet. They could be waiting for you at the next networking function or they could turn up as a customer walking into your place of business. The point is, you never know who could be the one to offer you suggestions that might open up the door to wider markets or coach you on how to retain and grow your customer base.

I'm sure by now you understand that to be successful in business it takes hard work and dedication. And there'll be times when you'll want to call it quits—throw in the towel. Those are the times when it's nice to have someone in your corner encouraging you to go on—someone who has walked in your entrepreneurial shoes and has seen the good and bad times. But they persevered and are here to stabilize you when you wobble—even catch you when you fall. They have the luxury of experience on their side and can tell when you're getting ready to veer off course. A mentor can introduce you to prospective clients or pass along a tip to help fend off the competition.

In Chapter 13, Marketing Research, we touched on the organization, SCORE, funded by the SBA. There are other organizations that can also assist you on your way up the entrepreneurial ladder. Small Business Development Centers (SBDC) are spread out in various locations throughout the country, including Alaska and Hawaii. These centers provide counseling and training in the areas of finance, marketing and management. You may need someone to look over your business plan before submitting it to a bank for resource capital. Or, maybe you're at a stalemate in the preparation of the plan; cash flow projections can be tough when you're a new venture. Or, maybe you need some assistance in the development stages, i.e.: how to go about finding and reaching your target market.

The SBDC offers a mentor/protégé program for all of those reasons and a lot more and their skill expertise runs the gamut from technology to manufacturing and service to retail. College students are also tapped to conduct research, while at the same time honing the skills and experience necessary for future career choices.

Contact your local SBA either by telephone or on-line to find the location of the SBDC nearest you.

## The Key to Success:

How you find your mentor is not important—what is important, is that you do. Take advantage of the knowledge that's available…remember what I said before about the roof and the shingle!

*"I run scared every business day and use every legal means necessary to survive and grow."*
—John H. Johnson

## Chapter 29
# Opening Day

Congratulations…you've come a long way! What began as a dream is now reality. You deserve to take another deep breath and savor the fruits of your challenging labor…but not for too long! You've still got some work to do. As a matter of fact, depending on how you look at it, the real work may have just begun. Only this time—you'll be working on your own terms, in your own shop and deciding your own salary.

Do you remember in Chapter 1 when I mentioned that we would come back to the meaning of an entrepreneur? Well, from all the knowledge you've gained after reading this guide and taking action to put it to use, has your definition changed at all?

Take a few minutes and write down what it means to be an entrepreneur now:

_____

_____

_____

_____

Is it the same as before or have you added or subtracted some words or sentences? Whatever you've written, stand by it, be proud of it and always believe in it.

Now, let's create a checklist for everything you might need before your open the doors to prosperity. Here are some of the most important things you'll need to do before you open for business:

▼ I know it may sound obvious, but check to make sure you have cash in the register if you're operating a storefront—all of those customers are sure to need change

▼ Test your office equipment, i.e.: computer, telephone, fax, copier, printer, and your Web-site, to make certain everything is in working order

▼ Give your suppliers (if you need them) one last call to firm up delivery dates

▼ If you're working from a storefront, take a last walk around the outside making sure your signage is displayed properly and inside your shelves are sufficiently stocked

▼ Always budget extra cash in your financial statement for unforeseeable expenses or unseen glitches…they seem to always creep up near opening day

▼ Remember to place ads announcing the opening and strategically pass out Grand Opening fliers

▼ Re-direct those opening-day jitters into a positive energy that will bring in customer sales and satisfaction

## The Key to Success:

And finally, you've done it—it's time to party! A Grand Opening Celebration! You are now a card-carrying member of the more than 20 million entrepreneurs controlling their personal and financial destinies.

# Appendix A
# Business Structures

Now, Let's review the types of Business Structures and decide which one fits you the best.

## Sole Proprietorship
Advantages:

▼ The least expensive and easiest business formation for entrepreneurs and small businesses.

▼ Generally a one-person operation.

▼ The owner has total control of the business

▼ You are taxed as an individual: Taxes are recorded on your Federal Tax 1040 form, and Schedule C—profit & loss form (you'll also need to file a Schedule SE—self employment tax form along with the 1040 and Schedule C)

## Disadvantages

▼ You face unlimited liability (your personal assets, i.e.: house or car are at risk of seizure)

▼ Raising capital will be difficult outside your own personal finances. Banks and Investment firms are reluctant to make loans to a sole proprietorship.

▼ Business ceases to exist upon the death of the owner

## Partnership
Advantages:

▼ A business relationship between two or more individuals sharing the operation and management responsibility of a business venture.

▼ Like Sole Proprietorships, Partnerships are easy to establish and less expensive than forming a corporation, however, having a formal partnership agreement to spell out responsibilities and resolve potential conflicts is highly recommended.

▼ Very little government regulation

▼ Partnerships comes in two flavors—General and Limited Partnerships: Under General Partnerships each partner is responsible for the management of the company and are liable for the debts of the firm. Under a Limited Partnership there are two types of partners: both general and limited. The general partners own and run the firm whereas the limited partners serve as investors only and have no control over everyday operations. They are also limited to losses equal to their investment in the partnership. (For new businesses it is far less complicated to form a general partnership.)

▼ Increased capital and skill pool

## Disadvantages:

▼ Partners are personally liable for the debts of the firm

▼ Unless stipulated in a partnership agreement—the partnership dissolves upon the death or withdrawal of a partner

▼ Each general partner can hire, fire, take out loans and make decisions that have an impact on all partners involved. (Choose your partners carefully)

# Limited Liability Company
## Advantages:

▼ An attractive alternative to forming a partnership or corporation

▼ Status as a legal entity—separate from its owners (similar to a corporation)

▼ Provides limited liability protection—personal assets are not at risk

▼ No limit to the number of owners

▼ 'Pass through' taxation: Income and losses are taxed at the individual rate and reported on members personal tax returns (no double taxation as with corporations)

## Disadvantages:

▼ More expensive to set up than a sole proprietorship or partnerships

▼ Still a relatively new business structure—laws vary from state to state

▼ Depending on the state where the LLC was formed—the business may dissolve upon the death, retirement or resignation of a member.

▼ The legality of an LLC business transaction in a state other than its own is dependent upon the laws governing that particular state

# 'C' Corporation
## Advantages:

▼ A legal business entity with rights and privileges separate from those of its owners (shareholders)

▼ Liable for all its debts

▼ Does not dissolve upon the death of the owner(s)

▼ Can sell stock to raise capital

▼ The corporation can own assets and borrow money

## Disadvantages:

▼ Can be complex and expensive to set up

▼ Subject to strenuous government regulations

▼ Double taxation—taxes paid on corporate earnings (Tax Form 1120) and again on dividends distributed to shareholders on personal tax returns

▼ Articles of incorporation must be filed through the Secretary of States office

▼ You'll more than likely require the services of an attorney for corporate formation

# Subchapter 'S' Corporation
## Advantages:

▼ No double taxation—similar to a partnership 'pass through' setup (income and losses are included on personal tax returns)

▼ Can have up to 75 shareholders or investors

▼ Limited personal liability

## Disadvantages:

▼ More complex and costly to setup than sole proprietorships or partnerships

▼ No more than 75 shareholders allowed

▼ The company must be incorporated in the U.S.

▼ To qualify as an 'S' Corporation, certain criteria must be satisfied in accordance to the state where the business is incorporated

▼ All shareholders must agree to the election of the 'S' corporation status

▼ Articles of incorporation must be filed through the Secretary of States office

# Appendix B
# Financial Resources

## African American Banks

Citizens Trust Bank
1700 3rd. Avenue North
Birmingham, AL 35203
(205) 328-2041

First Tuskegee Bank
301 North Elm Street
Tuskegee, AL 36083
(334) 262-0800

OneUnited Bank
3683 Crenshaw Blvd.
Los Angeles, CA 90016
(877) 663-8648

Independence Federal Savings Bank
1229 Connecticut Avenue, NW
Washington, DC 20036
(202) 628-5500

Industrial Bank, N.A.
4812 Georgia Avenue, NW
Washington, DC 20011
(202) 722-2022

OneUnited Bank
3275 NW 79th Street
Miami, FL 33147
(877) 663-8648

Capitol City Bank & Trust Company
562 Lee Street S.W.
Atlanta, GA 30310
(404) 752-6067

Citizens Trust Bank of Atlanta
75 Piedmont Avenue
Atlanta, GA 30303
(404) 653-2800

Highland Community Bank
1701 W. 87th Street
Chicago, IL 60620
(773) 881-6800

Dryades Savings Bank, FSB
231 Carondelet Street, Suite 200
New Orleans, LA 70130
(504) 581-5891

OneUnited Bank
133 Federal Street
Boston, MA 02110
(617) 457-4400
(877) 663-8648
www.oneunited.com

The Harbor Bank of Maryland
25 West Fayette Street
Baltimore, MD 21201
(410) 528-1800

First Independence National Bank
44 Michigan Avenue
Detroit, MI 48226
(313) 256-8400

Douglas National Bank
1670 E. 63rd Street
Kansas City, MO 64110
(913) 321-7200

City National Bank of New Jersey
900 Broad Street
Newark, NJ 07102
(973) 624-0865

Carver Federal Savings Bank
75 West 125th Street
New York, NY 10027
(212) 876-4747

American State Bank
3816 N. Peoria
Tulsa, OK 74106
(918) 428-2211

Albina Community Bank
2002 NE Martin Luther King, Jr. Blvd.
Portland, OR 97212
(503) 288-7280

United Bank of Philadelphia
714 Market Street
Philadelphia, PA 19106
(215) 829-2265

South Carolina Community Bank
P.O. Box 425
1545 Sumter Street
Columbia, SC 29202
(803) 733-8100

Tri State Bank of Memphis
180 South Main
Memphis, TN 38103
(901) 525-0384

First State Bank
445 Mount Cross Road
Danville, VA 24543
(434) 797-3929

Consolidated Bank and Trust Company
320 North First Street
Richmond, VA 23219
(804) 771-5200

North Milwaukee State Bank
5630 West Fond du Lac Avenue
Milwaukee, WI 53216
(414) 466-2344

## Financing Resources:

SBA—(listing of Small Business Friendly Banks by State)
www.sbaonline.sba.gov

Count-Me-In (for Women's Economic Independence)
(212) 691-6262
www.count-me-in.org

The Abilities Fund (Financing, training and technical assistance for the disabled)
www.abilitiesfund.org

American Express Community Business Card
www.americanexpress.com/smallbusiness

## Accounting Resources:

American Accounting Association
5717 Bessie Drive
Sarasota, FL 34233
(941) 921-7747
www.aaahq.org

The American Institute of Certified Public Accountants
www.aicpa.org

Independent Accountants International
(305) 670-0580
www.accountants.org

## Accounting Software:

QuickBooks (Intuit)
2632 Marine Way (Headquarters location)
Mountain View, CA 94043
(888) 729-1996
www.intuit.com or www.quickbooks.com

MYOB US, Inc.
300 Roundhill Drive
Rockaway, NJ 07866
(800) 322-6962 or (973) 586-2200
www.myob.com

Peachtree Software
1505 Pavilion Place
Norcross, GA 30093
(800) 247-3224 or (770) 724-4000
www.peachtree.com

Microsoft Small Business Manager
Microsoft bCentral
Redmond, WA 98052-6399
(866) 223-6872
www.bcentral.com

DacEasy (Best Software-Small Business Division)
1505 Pavilion Place
Norcross, GA 30093
(866) 297-2088
www.daceasy.com

# Appendix C
# Business Resources

## African American Insurance Companies

Atlanta Life Insurance Company
100 Auburn Avenue N.E.
Atlanta, GA 30303
(404) 659-2100

Reliable Life Insurance Company
718 Jackson Street
Monroe, LA 71210
(318) 387-1000

Golden State Mutual Life Insurance Co.
1999 West Adams Blvd.
Los Angeles, CA 90018
(213) 731-1131

Protective Industrial Insurance Company
2300 11th Avenue North
Birmingham, AL 35234
(205) 323-5256

North Carolina Mutual Life
Insurance Co.
411 West Chapel Hill Street
Durham, NC 27701
(919) 682-9201

## General Insurance Contacts

Health Insurance Association of America
1201 F Street NW, Suite 500
Washington, DC 20004-1204
(202) 824-1600
www.hiaa.org

Small Business Service Bureau
(Insurance)
(800) 343-0939
www.sbsb.com

## Government Contacts

U.S. Census Bureau
4700 Silver Hill Road
Suitland, MD 20746
(301) 763-3316
www.census.gov/csd/mwb

U.S. Department of Commerce
14th St. and Constitution Ave. NW
Washington, DC 20230
(202) 482-5270
www.doc.gov

Internal Revenue Service
1111 Constitution Ave. NW
Washington, DC 20224
(202) 622-5000
www.irs.gov

U.S. Patent and Trademark Office
2021 South Clark Place
Crystal Plaza 3
Arlington, VA 22202
(800) 786-9199
www.uspto.gov

U.S. Small Business Administration
(SBA)
409 Third St. SW
Washington, DC 20416
(800) 827-5722 or (202) 205-6770
www.sba.gov

U.S. Department of Labor
200 Constitution Ave. NW
Room S-1032
Washington, DC 20210
(202) 693-4650
www.dol.gov

U.S. Chamber of Commerce
(202) 463-5570
www.uschamber.org

U.S. Chamber of Commerce Small
Business Institute
1615 H. St. NW
Washington, DC 20062
(800) 835-4730
www.usccsbi.com

Bureau of Economic Analysis
www.bea.doc.gov &
www.polisci.com/exec/commerce

Bureau of Labor Statistics
2 Massachusetts Avenue NE
Washington, DC 20212
(202) 606-5886
www.bls.gov

National SCORE Office
409 Third St. SW
Washington, DC 20024
(800) 634-0245
www.score.org

U.S. Securities and Exchange
Commission
450 Fifth St. NW
Washington, DC 20549
(202) 942-7040
www.sec.gov

Export-Import Bank of the U.S.
811 Vermont Ave. NW
Washington, DC 20571
(800) 565-3946
www.exim.gov

U.S. Copyright Office (Library of
Congress)
101 Independence Ave. SE
Washington, DC 20559
(202) 707-3000
www.loc.gov/copyright

U.S. Printing Office
North Capital and 8th St.
Washington, DC 20402
(202) 512-1800
www.access.gpo.gov

U.S. Food and Drug Administration
(FDA)
5600 Fishers Lane
Rockville, MD 20857
(888) 463-6332
www.fda.gov

# Business Associations/Organizations

The Association for Enterprise Opportunity (AEO)
1601 North Kent Street, Suite 1101
Arlington, VA 22209
(703) 841-7760
www.microenterpriseworks.org

Minority Business Development Agency
14th St. and Constitution Ave.
Washington, DC 20230
(202) 482-5061
www.mbda.org

National Association of Home-Based Businesses
10451 Mill Run Circle, Suite 400
Owings Mills, MD 21117
(800) 228-0810 or (410) 363-3698
www.usahomebusiness.com

American Association of Home-Based Businesses
P.O. Box 10023
Rockville, MD 20849
(800) 447-9710
www.aahbb.org

Association of Small Business Development Centers
3108 Columbia Pike, Suite 300
Arlington, VA 22204
(703) 271-8700
www.asbdc-us.org

National Black Business Trade Association
P.O. Box 75022
Washington, DC 20013
(321) 946-2486
www.nbbta.org

National Association of Black Women Entrepreneurs, Inc.
P.O. Box 311299
Detroit, MI 48231
(313) 203-3379

Professional Women in Business
P.O. Box 513494
Los Angeles, CA 90051
(310) 669-4723

Urban Financial Services Coalition
1300 L. Street NW, Suite 825
Washington, DC 20005
(202) 289-8335
www.ufscnet.org

National Bankers Association
1513 P. Street NW
Washington, DC 20005
(202) 588-5432
www.nationalbankers.org

National Association for the Self Employed
P.O. Box 612067
DFW Airport
Dallas, TX 75261-2067
(800) 232-6273
www.nase.org

National Federation of Independent Business (NFIB)
600 Maryland Ave. SW, Suite 700
Washington, DC 20024
(800) 634-2669 or (202) 554-9000
www.nfibonline.com

National Association of Small Business Investment Companies
666 11th Street NW, # 750
Washington, DC 20001
(202) 628-5055
www.nasbic.org

iVillage
www.ivillage.com/topics/work

Small Office Home Office
www.soho.org

Collection of Small Business Resources
www.towbrick.com

Smart Business Supersite
www.smartbiz.com

National Black Business Council
(888) 264-6222
www.nbbc.org

International Black Buyers & Manufacturers Expo & Conference
312 Florida Avenue NW
Washington, DC 20001
(202) 797-9070
www.ibbmec.com

National Black Chamber of Commerce
2000 L. St. NW, Suite 200
Washington, DC 20036
(202) 466-6888
www.nationalbcc.org

National Federation of Black Women Business Owners
(202) 833-3450

National Minority Supplier Development Council (NMSDC)
1040 Avenue of the Americas, 2nd Floor
New York, NY 10018
(212) 944-2430
www.nmsdcus.org

8(a) Sources
www.sba8a.com/nmsdc

National Association of Women Business Owners (NAWBO)
8405 Greenboro Drive, Suite 800
McLean, VA 22102
(800) 556-2926 or (703) 506-3268
www.nawbo.org

National Foundation for Women Business Owners (NFWBO)
(Center for Women's Business Research)
1411 K Street NW, Suite 1350
Washington, DC 20005-3407
(202) 638-3060
www.nfwbo.org

American Association of Minority Businesses
537 W. Sugar Creek Road, Suite 104
Charlotte, NC 28213
(704) 376-2262
www.website1.com/aamb

Small Office Home Office Association International
1767 Business Center Drive, Suite 450
Reston, VA 20190
(703) 438-3000
www.sohoa.com

The Encyclopedia of Associations
(Gale Research, Inc.)
362 Lakeside Drive
Foster City, CA 94404
(800) 877-4253
www.library.dialog.com

## Franchise Information Services

International Franchise Association
1350 New York Ave. NW, Suite 900
Washington, DC 20005
(202) 628-8000
www.franchise.org

American Franchisee Association
53 West Jackson Blvd., Suite 205
Chicago, IL 60604
(312) 431-0545
www.franchisee.org

American Association of Franchisees
and Dealers
P.O. Box 81887
San Diego, CA 92138-1887
(800) 733-9858 or (619) 235-2556
www.aafd.org

Franchise Finance Corporation of
America
17207 North Perimeter Drive
Scottsdale, AZ 85255
(602) 585-4500
www.ffca.com

International Franchise Capital
3900 Fifth Avenue, Suite 340
San Diego, CA 92103
(619) 260-6000
www.franchiseloan.com

Franchise Works
www.franchiseworks.com

Franchise Solutions
www.franchisesolutions.com

## Web-site Designers & Domain Names

USA Web Designers Directory
www.digitalspinner.com

Suppleblue, Inc.
www.suppleblue.com

Register.Com
www.register.com

## Marketing Research & Data Companies

The Dun & Bradstreet Corporation
(Headquarter Location)
103 JFK Parkway
Short Hills, NJ 07078
(973) 921-5500
www.dnb.com

Dun & Bradstreet Inc.
3 Sylvan Way
Parsippany, NJ 07054
(800) 526-0651 or 800 234-3867
www.dnb.com

Thomas Publishing Companies
One Penn Plaza
New York, NY 10
(212) 290-7200
www.thomasregister.com

Gale Research Corporation (Thompson/Gale)
www.gale.com or www.galegroup.com

National Small Business United
1156 15th St. NW, Suite 1100
Washington, DC 20005
(202) 293-8830
www.nsbu.org

Marketing Research Association
1344 Silas Deane Hwy, #306
Rocky Hill, CT 06067
(860) 257-4008
www.mra-net.org

Hoover's Online
www.hoovers.com

Industry Snapshot Report
www.integrainfo.com

U.S.A. Data
www.usadata.com

## Marketing/ Direct Marketing/ Direct Mailing Resources:

American Marketing Association
250 South Wacker Drive, Suite 200
Chicago, IL 60606
(312) 648-0536
www.ama.org

Direct Marketing Association
1120 Avenue of the Americas
New York, NY 10036
(212) 768-7277
www.the-dma.org

Public Relations Society of America
33 Irving Place
New York, NY 10003
(212) 995-2230
www.prsa.org

Think Direct Marketing
www.thinkdirectmarketing.com

List Bazaar
www.listbaazar.com

Association of National Advertisers
708 Third Ave.
New York, NY 10017
(212) 697-5950
www.ana.net

National Mail Order Association
2807 Polk St. NE
Minneapolis, MN 55418
(612) 788-1673
www.nmoa.org

Zairmail Express Direct
www.zairmail.com

United States Postal Service
www.usps.com

## Trade / Trade Show Companies:

International Trade Administration
www.ita.doc.gov

Trade Show News Network
www.tsnn.com

Ameribiz Global Business & Trade
www.ameribiz.com

Trade Show Central
www.tscentral.com

## Business Broker Resources: (Buying or Selling Businesses)

International Business Brokers Associations
11250 Roger Bacon Drive, Suite 8
Reston, VA 20190
(703) 437-7464
www.ibba.org

The U.S. Business Exchange (USBX)
www.usbx.com

BizBuySell
www.bizbuysell.com

VR Business Brokers
www.vrbusinessbrokers.com

National Insurance Consumer
Helpline / Insurance Information
Institute
110 William Street
New York, NY 10036
(800) 942-4242
www.iii.org

## Legal Information & Services

Nolo-Law for All
www.nolo.com

Lexis-Nexis
www.lexis-nexis.com

American Bar Association
750 North Lake Shore Drive
Chicago, IL 60611
(312) 988-5000
www.abanet.org

Business Law
http://businesslaw.gov

## Legal Software:

Quicken Lawyer Home and Small
Business Legal Suite

Quicken Legal Business Pro 2004

Kiplinger's Home and Business
Attorney

# The Nation's Top 30 Franchises

Thousands of prospective entrepreneurs seeking stability in unstable times have turned to franchising. It offers the perks of a corporation and the freedom of entrepreneurship.

If you believe this is your year to buy a franchise, *Entrepreneur*'s 25th Annual Franchise 500® is a great place to start your search.

Use the list solely as a research tool to compare franchise operations. It has been compiled, based on numerous factors, including: financial strength and stability, growth rate and size of the system, as well as the number of years in business and length of time franchising, start-up costs, litigation, percentage of terminations and whether the company provides financing. Financial data was audited by an independent CPA firm.

Always conduct your own independent investigation before you invest money in a franchise. Read the related materials carefully; get help from an attorney and a CPA in reviewing any legal documents; talk to as many existing franchisees as possible, and visit their outlets. The best way to protect yourself is to do your homework.

| | |
|---|---|
| 1 Subway—Submarine sandwiches & salads | $86K-213K |
| 2 Curves—Women's fitness & weight-loss centers | $35.6K-41.1K |
| 3 Quizno's Franchise Co.—The Submarine sandwiches, soups, salads | $208.4K-243.8K |
| 4 7-Eleven Inc.—Convenience store | Varies |
| 5 Jackson Hewitt Tax Service—Tax preparation services | $47.4K-75.2K |
| 6 The UPS Store—Postal/business/communications services | $141.1K-239.7K |
| 7 McDonald's—Hamburgers, chicken, salads | $506K-1.6M |
| 8 Jani-King—Commercial cleaning | $11.3K-34.1K+ |
| 9 Dunkin' Donuts—Donuts & baked goods | $255.7K-1.1M |

| | | |
|---|---|---|
| 10 | Baskin-Robbins USA Co.—Ice cream & yogurt | $145.7K-527.8K |
| 11 | Jiffy Lube Int'l. Inc.—Fast oil change | $174K-194K |
| 12 | InterContinental Hotels Group—Hotels | Varies |
| 13 | Sonic Drive In Restaurants—Drive-in restaurant | $710K-2.3M |
| 14 | Domino's Pizza LLC—Pizza, buffalo wings, breadsticks | $141.4K-415.1K |
| 15 | Super 8 Motels Inc.—Economy motels | $291K-2.3M |
| 16 | Kumon Math & Reading Centers—Supplemental education | $8K-30K |
| 17 | Chem-Dry Carpet Drapery & Upholstery Cleaning Carpet, drapery & upholstery cleaning | $23.6K-82.8K |
| 18 | ServiceMaster Clean—Commercial/residential cleaning & disaster restoration | $26.6K-90.5K |
| 19 | RE/MAX Int'l. Inc.—Real estate | $20K-200K |
| 20 | Snap-on Tools—Professional tools & equipment | $17.6K-254.7K |
| 21 | Burger King Corp.—Hamburgers, fries, breakfast & other items | $294K-2.8M |
| 22 | Jan-Pro Franchising Int'l. Inc.—Commercial cleaning | $1K-14K+ |
| 23 | Merle Norman Cosmetics—Cosmetics studios | $33.1K-162K |
| 24 | Papa John's Int'l. Inc.—Pizza | $250K |
| 25 | Jazzercise Inc.—Dance/exercise classes | $2.6K-32.8K |
| 26 | RadioShack—Consumer electronics | $60K |
| 27 | Days Inns Worldwide Inc.—Hotels & inns | $400K-5.4M |
| 28 | Liberty Tax Service—Income-tax preparation services | $38.1K-49.1K |
| 29 | Midas Auto Service Experts—Auto repair & maintenance services | $379.4K-528K |
| 30 | Dairy Queen—Soft-serve dairy products/sandwiches | $655K-1.3M |

# Entrepreneurial Workbook

You've read and re-read the book and have a good understanding about how you'd like to take financial control of your life and shape your future. This can be your defining moment. Copy the following pages. (You may do this exercise as often as you feel the need to update). List your strengths, your weaknesses, your skills, and finally…your interests. Take your time; think about your statements and be honest.

## My Strengths
(Nobody does it better!)

1)_____

_____

_____

_____

2)_____

_____

_____

_____

3)_____

_____

_____

_____

4)_____

_____

_____

_____

5)_____

_____

_____

_____

## My Weaknesses
(Things I would absolutely love to steer clear of!)

1)_____

_____

_____

_____

2)_____

_____

_____

_____

3)_____

_____

_____

_____

4) _____

_____

_____

_____

5) _____

_____

_____

_____

## My Skills

1) _____

_____

_____

_____

2) _____

_____

_____

_____

3) _____

_____

_____

_____

4)_____

_____

_____

_____

5)_____

_____

_____

_____

## My Interests

1)_____

_____

_____

_____

2)_____

_____

_____

_____

3)_____

_____

_____

_____

4)_____

_____

_____

_____

5)_____

_____

_____

_____

# Compare & Contrast

| Skill Strengths |
|---|
| 1. |
| 2. |
| 3. |
| 4. |
| 5. |
| 6. |
| 7. |
| 8. |
| 9. |
| 10. |

| Skill Weaknesses |
|---|
| 1. |
| 2. |
| 3. |
| 4. |
| 5. |
| 6. |
| 7. |
| 8. |
| 9. |
| 10. |

| Interests |
|---|
| 1. |
| |
| 2. |
| |
| 3. |
| |
| 4. |
| |
| 5. |
| |

## Business Examples and Ratings

| Heading | Skill | Rating |
|---|---|---|
| Landscape architect | gardening | 2 |
| Consultant | small business marketing | 3 |
| Baker | holiday cakes | 3 |
|  |  |  |
|  |  |  |
|  |  |  |
|  |  |  |
|  |  |  |
|  |  |  |
|  |  |  |
|  |  |  |
|  |  |  |
|  |  |  |

1 = Exposed—You may want to research the industry more thoroughly before making a decision.

2 = Experienced—You may need to brush up on your skills before deciding on self-employment

3 = Expert—Great chance at entrepreneurial readiness!

## Business Possibilities
(What I Can Do With My Skills, Interests & Experience)

1._____

_____

2._____

_____

3._____

_____

4._____

_____

5._____

_____

6._____

_____

7._____

_____

8._____

_____

9._____

_____

10._____

_____

# Timeline
(Now it's time to bring your plan to completion)

| Task | Start Date | Completion Date |
|---|---|---|
|  |  |  |
|  |  |  |
|  |  |  |
|  |  |  |
|  |  |  |
|  |  |  |
|  |  |  |
|  |  |  |
|  |  |  |
|  |  |  |
|  |  |  |
|  |  |  |
|  |  |  |
|  |  |  |

Congratulations on Your New Business!

## Notes:

*"If we have the courage and tenacity of our forebears, who stood firmly like a rock against the lash of slavery, we shall find a way to do for our day what they did for theirs."*
—Mary McLeod Bethune

## Appendix F
# African-American Entrepreneurs Who Have Made a Difference

Oftentimes, the ultimate goal of an entrepreneur is to leave a legacy and to help others less fortunate than they. In short, they are destined to make a difference. With a dream, desire and determination, you too can leave your mark in history and make a difference to the many people who will get to know and understand your personal story.

## Benjamin Banneker

Benjamin Banneker was an astronomer, farmer, mathematician, and surveyor. In 1791, he was a technical to Major Andrew Ellicott, the surveyor appointed by President George Washington to lay out the boundaries of the Federal District, which is now Washington, D.C. Secretary of State Thomas Jefferson had recommended Banneker for this work.

Banneker was born in Maryland on November 9, 1731. His father and grandfather were former slaves. His grandmother, an Englishwoman, taught him to read and write. For several winters he attended a small racially integrated school. There he developed a keen interest in mathematics and science.

Later, while farming, Banneker pursued his mathematical studies and taught himself astronomy. In 1753, he completed a clock built entirely of wood, each gear carved by hand. His only models were a pocket watch and a picture of a clock. The clock kept almost perfect time for over 50 years.

From 1791 to 1796, Banneker began the study of astronomy and was soon predicting future solar and lunar eclipses, making all the astronomical and tide calculations and weather predictions for a yearly almanac, which became a top seller from Pennsylvania to Virginia and even into Kentucky.

Banneker sent Thomas Jefferson a copy of his first almanac. With it he sent a letter calling for the abolition of slavery and a liberal attitude toward African-Americans. Banneker' s skills impressed Jefferson, who sent a copy of the almanac to the Royal Academy of Sciences in Paris as evidence that African Americans were not intellectually inferior to European Americans.

Banneker died on Sunday, October 9, 1806 at the age of 74. A few small memorial traces still exist in the Ellicott City/Oella region of Maryland, where Banneker spent his entire life except for the Federal survey. In 1980, the U.S. Postal Service issued a postage stamp in his honor.

## Don H. Barden

Don H. Barden, who heads the Majestic Star Casino in Gary, Indiana is one of the nation's leading African-American entrepreneurs.

Barden, whose journey to success began when he was one of thirteen children living in Detroit, now owns a syndicate of businesses. He is owner, Chairman and Chief Executive Officer of the Barden Companies, Inc., the Majestic Star Casino, Waycor Development Company and the Namibia, Africa-based Barden International, Inc. His international conglomerate of operations covers a wide variety of industries, including the casino, real estate development, entertainment, automotive sales, service and manufacturing.

Barden has made history in the casino business, In December 2001, he broadened his entrepreneurial reach by acquiring Fitzgerald's Casino Hotel with properties in Las Vegas, Mississippi and Colorado. With four casinos, Barden is the first African-American to wholly own a national casino company.

Majestic Star now operates in three of the top five gaming markets in the United States. The casino has approximately 4,500 slots, 110 game tables, 1,145 hotel rooms and 3,800 employees.

Under Barden's guidance, Barden Companies and its affiliates have seen earnings soar from to revenues of more than $347 million in 2003, which has catapulted him into the ranks of one of the largest African-American owned businesses in the country and one of the most respected enterprises worldwide.

Over the past 30 years, Mr. Barden has successfully developed, owned and operated many business enterprises in various industries including real estate development, casino gaming, broadcasting, cable television and international trade. In 2003, Black Enterprise Magazine selected Mr. Barden as Company of the Year. In 2004, Mr. Barden received the Trumpet Award for Entrepreneur of the Year.

## Emma C. Chappell

Emma Chappell grew up in West Philadelphia, a black working-class neighborhood. Her mother died when she was fourteen; her father, a chef raised her. Her first thoughts were to become a nurse, but because of her high math aptitude, she was encouraged by her pastor, Reverend Leon Sullivan to instead pursue a job at a bank. She entered the banking industry with her first job as a clerk-photographer for Continental Bank, earning $45 a week while attending college. Chappell received a B.S. at Temple University and a Graduate Degree in banking and finance at Stonier School at Rutgers University.

It was Chappell's credentials as a banker and community leader that led a group of African-American business owners and investment bankers in 1987 to make her an offer she couldn't refuse-to create her own bank. There was a need and an opportunity for a black commercial bank in Philadelphia and they were willing to put up the seed money, but needed a bank manager, who had experience as well as credibility in the African-American community.

Chappell along with 12 other cofounders—United's board of directors— contributed about $600,000 in start-up money to cover the cost of a business plan and feasibility study. The group set out to raise $3 million in capital, the amount needed to become a state-chartered commercial bank. In her quest for capital, Chappell was able to net over $1 million from Mellon Bank, Corestates Financial Corp., Meridian Bancorp., First Fidelity Bancorp., PNC Bank (formerly Provident National Bank) and Continental Bank. Other moneys came from insurance companies and corporations.

With the 1987 stock market crash, the group's strategy of raising the capital entirely from institutional investors fell through; the bank now had to raise $5 million to be fully capitalized. The state granted a conditional charter allowing United to sell stock: $10 a share in blocks of 50 and multiples of $500 and for the next three years, Chappell raised the necessary money as well as the community's financial consciousness. She even held Black Bank Sunday where some 200 pastors across the city announced from the pulpit that the bank was just $1 million short of meeting its goal. A citywide congregation raised $400,000 that day. (The stock was registered in the church's name.) When the votes were in and the money was counted that April of 1991, some 14 institutions had given $2.7 million and about 3,000 individuals most of them first-time investors, who purchased shares of stock in blocks of $500. had raised $3.3 million. After a tough, uphill five-year campaign, Chappell saw United Bank's doors officially open on March 23, 1992. It is Philadelphia's only African-American-controlled commercial bank. United Bank of Philadelphia has four branch offices in urban Philadelphia.

## D. William E. Cox

Dr. William E. Cox is the president and co-founder of Cox, Matthews & Associates, Inc. (CMA), a firm specializing in publishing, satellite television production, training and consulting, with offices in both Fairfax, Virginia and New York City. His *Black Issues Book Review*, the nation's foremost magazine about and for African Americans in publishing, was founded in 1999.

Dr. Cox's education credentials include a doctorate in higher education administration from the George Washington University and master's degrees in both counseling psychology and public administration from Ball State University. He earned his undergraduate degree from Alabama A & M University. Bill has also taken both graduate and post-graduate courses at the college of William and Mary, Harvard University and the University of Nevada–Las Vegas.

Dr. Cox has received numerous prestigious awards, including the Distinguished Leadership Award from the National Association for Equal Opportunity in Higher Education and he was inducted into the International Adult and Continuing Education Hall of Fame in 2000.

# Mel Farr

Mel Farr, All-American and All-Pro running back, shot to the top of the African American business world when the Mel Farr Auto Group grossed a staggering $596.6 million in 1998. Farr was born November 3, 1944, in Beaumont, Texas to Miller Farr, Sr. and Doretha Farr.

A natural athlete, Farr excelled in baseball, basketball, track and football. It was football that captured Farr's imagination; he was widely recruited from Hebert High School before choosing the University of California, Los Angeles. At UCLA, Farr was a consensus All-American from 1963 to 1967. He was also NFL Rookie of the Year in 1967 with the Detroit Lions and made the All-Pro team in 1967 and 1972. Plagued by injuries, Farr retired in 1973, ready to make the transition from football hero to businessman.

Determined to have a career beyond the gridiron, Farr completed his degree at the University of Detroit while still in the NFL. He worked during the off-season for the Ford Motor Company in its management program. In 1975, Mel Farr Ford opened in Oak Park, Michigan. Targeting the inner-city population with its high credit risk and need for automobiles and ready financing, Farr employed a variety of creative marketing and management approaches. Purchasing additional dealerships beginning in 1986, Farr's empire grew to more than thirteen dealerships and a 7-Up bottling plant. By 1998, the Mel Farr Auto Group was the top African American business in the country and the thirty-third-largest auto dealership in the United States.

# George Fraser

George Fraser is the author of two books, including the critically acclaimed bestseller, *Success Runs In Our Race; The Complete Guide to Effective Networking in the African American Community.* He is also the creator and publisher of the award winning *Success Guide, The Networking Guide to Black Resources.* Over the last nine years, twenty versions of Success Guide have been published for nine different cities, across America. He is a frequent contributor to scholarly journals on a wide range of topics to include business ethics and economic development. His book *Race For Success; The Ten Best Business Opportunities For Blacks In America* was published in February 1998, by the William Morrow Company.

Mr. Fraser attended New York University and received his executive training at the Amos Tuck School of Business at Dartmouth College.

Mr. Fraser spent 17 years in management with Procter & Gamble, United Way and Ford. Today as a popular speaker and author he has appeared on more than 150 television and radio talk shows. His views are solicited by media as diverse as CNN and the Wall Street Journal. He speaks nearly 150 times per year all around the world, and is considered by most to be one of the foremost authorities on networking and building effective relationships.

## Willie Gary

One of the 11 children of Turner and Mary Gary, Willie Gary was born in 1947 in Eastman, Georgia and raised in migrant farm communities in Florida, Georgia and the Carolinas. Willie "the giant killer" Gary beat the odds to become a multi-millionaire nationally renowned attorney, who is known for giving back to the less fortunate.

Gary took his credentials as a Florida All-State High School football player to Shaw University in Raleigh, North Carolina, where he received an athletic scholarship and co-captained the team during the 1969, 1970 and 1971 seasons. He was the first African-American male to go to college from the small town of Indiantown where his family labored in the cane fields. Earning a Bachelor's degree in business administration, he continued on the North Carolina Central University in Durham where he earned a Juris Doctorate in 1974. Gary moved back to Stuart where he was admitted to the Florida Bar and opened the first black law firm in Martin County. Gloria, his childhood sweetheart, now wife, assisted him at this newly formed law firm.

Since then, Mr. Gary's practice has grown into the thriving national partnership known as Gary, Williams, Parenti, Finney, Lewis, McManus, Watson & Sperando. The firm is made up of 34 attorneys, a team of paralegals, a professional staff of 90 including in-house General Counsel, six nurses, two full-time investigators, an administrator, a certified public accountant, a public relations director, as well as a full administrative staff. Willie Gary has represented little known clients against major corporations and he has won some of the biggest jury awards in U.S. history, including more than 150 cases valued well in excess of a million dollars each.

*Forbes Magazine* has listed him as one of the top 50 attorneys in the United States. He has also been profiled as Person of the Week on ABC's World News Tonight with Peter Jennings, focused on Lifestyles of the Rich and Famous, made a guest appearance on the Oprah Winfrey Show, and appeared on CBS evening news Eye on America segment with Dan Rather.

Mr. Gary also owns his won national television cable network, which is based in Atlanta, Georgia. He is Chairman and CEO of Major Broadcasting Cable Network, or MBC. He is well known as a businessman, churchman, humanitarian and philanthropist who is deeply involved in charity and civic work. He is committed to enhancing the lives of young children through education and drug prevention and has formed the Gary Foundation to carry out this formidable task.

Mr. Gary has received numerous awards for his generosity and philanthropic endeavors, including: he Golden Trumpet Award from Turner Broadcasting Company and the prestigious Horatio Alger Award.

## Berry Gordy

Founder and owner of the Tamla-Motown family record labels, Berry Gordy, Jr., established Motown Records as one of the most important independent labels in the early '60s. Assembling an industrious staff of songwriters, producers, and musicians, Motown Records built one of the most impressive rosters of artist in the history of pop music and became the largest and most successful independent record company in the United States by 1964.

Born in 1929, Berry was the seventh child born to Berry and Bertha Gordy, an ambitious middle-class family with roots in Georgia farming and retailing. They had moved to Detroit in the 1922 where they established a successful painting and construction business that allowed the family to purchase a commercial building, which housed their Booker T. Washington grocery store. After studying business in college, Bertha co-founded the Friendship Mutual Life Insurance Company

Berry Gordy dropped out of school in the eleventh grade to become a professional boxer. He ended a respectable career as a featherweight in 1950, and after serving in the Army in Korea o opened up the 3-D Record Mart—House of Jazz. Married with three children, Berry, later, went to work on the assembly line at Ford's Lincoln-Mercury plant; but, 1957, he had quit that job to become a professional songwriter. He soon began to write songs for the artists that the owner of the Flame Show Bar managed and doing some of the producing. During this time he met Raynoma, who helped him write hit records…they would eventually be married.

Berry Gordy, Jr. the son of an African-American entrepreneur who hoped for the upward mobility of blacks, had found his niche. While he groomed and cultivated streetwise teens from the streets of Detroit to make them acceptable to Mainstream America, he made hit records that would impact the music of the world…forever.

In July 1988 Berry Gordy sold Motown Records to MCA and Boston Ventures for $61 million. Boston Ventures later bought out MCA's interest and sold Motown Records to the Dutch-based Polygram conglomerate for $325 million in 1993. In late 1994, Warner Books published Gordy's self-serving biography *To Be Loved.*

Berry Gordy was inducted into the Rock and Roll Hall of Fame in 1990.

## Earl Graves

Earl G. Graves was raised in the Bedford Stuyvesant section of New York, where he learned hard work and perseverance from his parents, Earl Goodwin and Winnaford Colette Sealy Graves. After receiving a B.A. in economics from Morgan State University he served two years in the Army, followed by a three-year stint as Senator Robert F. Kennedy's administrative assistant. After Kennedy's assassination, Graves entered the business arena, where he was to realize unprecedented success.

Since founding Black Enterprise in 1970, Graves has been named one of the ten most outstanding minority businessmen in the country by the president of the United States and received the National Award of Excellence in recognition of his achievements in minority business enterprise. Black Enterprise is recognized as the definitive resource for African American business professionals, entrepreneurs and policymakers in the public and private sectors.

Graves is president and CEO of Earl G. Graves, Ltd., parent corporation of the Earl G. Graves Publishing Company, which publishes Black Enterprise.

He has also served as chairman and CEO of Pepsi-Cola of Washington, D.C., the largest minority-controlled Pepsi-Cola franchise in the country. Since selling the franchise back to the parent company in 1998, Graves has continued to remain active with the company.

## Raymond Haysbert

Prominent Baltimore businessman Raymond Haysbert was born in a slum in Cincinnati in 1920. Haysbert was the fourth of eight children, and three of his younger siblings died while he was still a child. His father moved away when he was eight years old, and with the Depression following soon after, Haysbert and his three brothers soon went to work. He continued with school, and after graduating he enlisted in an ROTC program at Wilberforce University in Ohio. Haysbert was force to drop out of school his third year to make money, and when World War II broke out, he joined up with the Tuskegee Airman in Italy.

After returning from the war, Haysbert married his college sweetheart, Carol Roberts, to whom he had been introduced by Henry Parks in 1952. Parks had opened up his Baltimore sausage factory only a year before, and was struggling to make a go of it in an environment filled with bigotry. Haysbert and Parks partnered and began selling Parks Sausage throughout Baltimore, delivering fresh sausages daily to stores. The strategy was a success, and by 1955 Parks Sausage was a sponsor of the World Series. The company, which had reported losses in its first two years in existence, was reporting gross annual profits of $6 million by 1966 and $9 million in 1968. Parks Sausage became the first black-owned company to go public in 1969.

Following on his successes, Haysbert was named president of the company in 1974, and when the company was sold to a conglomerate in 1977, he made more than $1 million. By the mid-1980s, Parks Sausage was making almost $30 million a year, and Haysbert was serving on several boards of directors, including on the Baltimore Federal Reserve. After a heart attack in 1994, Haysbert handed over the presidency to his son, Reginald, but remained on as CEO. At that same time, he bought back the 49 percent of the company owned by Sara Lee, making Haysbert a 97.5 percent owner of the company, which was sold in 1995.

## Cathy Hughes

Cathy Hughes has been Chairperson of the Board of Directors and Secretary of Radio One and was Chief Executive Officer of Radio One from 1980 to 1997. She has worked in various capacities for Radio One including President, General Manager, General Sales Manager and talk show host. Hughes began her career in radio as General Sales Manager of WHUR-FM, the Howard University-owned, urban-contemporary radio station.

Hughes was turned down by 32 banks before securing a loan to buy her first radio station. She bought WOL-AM with a $1.5 million loan; SYNCOM was the lead investor and Chemical Bank was the senior lender. Today, Radio One is worth about $2 billion.

Born Catherine Elizabeth Woods, she attended Creighton University and the University of Nebraska at Omaha but did not graduate. Around 1969 she began working at KOWH, a black radio station in Omaha and her popularity prompted the School of Communications at Howard University in Washington, DC, offered her a job as lecturer. In 1973 she became sales director at WHUR-FM. Two years later Cathy Hughes became the station's general manager, boosting sales revenue to $3.5 million from $300,000. In 1979, she and her husband, Dewey Hughes, purchased a small Washington radio station, WOL, creating Radio One. When her marriage ended, she bought her husband's share in the station.

With twenty-seven stations in nine major markets, Radio One became the nation's largest black-owned radio chain. Cathy Hughes is the first African-American woman to head a firm publicly traded on a stock exchange in the United States; and in 1999 her IPO represented the largest broadcast corporation and the 16th-largest media company in the United States. In Jan. 2004, her company launched a new cable channel, TV One, aimed at African Americans.

## Hal Jackson

Born in 1915, in Charleston, South Carolina, Hal Jackson became one of the most important radio personalities of all time. He is a Founder, Owner and Group Chairman of Inner City Broadcasting Corporation, the largest privately held African American-owned broadcasting network in the nation, which includes: WBLS-FM 107.5 and WLIB in New York City, as well as fifteen other radio station outlets in major markets and cable television stations throughout the United States.

When Jackson was eight, both his parents died. After living with his sisters and other relatives, he moved out on his own in 1928 at the age of thirteen. Two years later, he moved north, settling in Washington, D.C. He attended Howard University, where his interests in sports and broadcasting grew. By the late 1930s, Jackson was an announcer for Howard University and Griffith Stadium.

In 1939, Jackson approached WINX in Washington, D.C. and proposed a radio show. Management flatly refused. Undeterred, Jackson purchased airtime through a wholesale buyer. He interviewed pioneering African Americans during his talk and music program, highlighting achievements of the community. His show proved so popular that, within six months, Jackson was able to buy airtime and sell ads on three additional stations in different cities. At the end of that year, he moved to New York with his radio show, The House that Jack Built. By the mid-1950s, he was again working at multiple stations. As the first African American announcer on network radio, he attracted the largest radio audience in the world at that time.

Through the years, Jackson has participated in numerous history-making events. He also founded Hal Jackson's Talented Teens International, a scholarship competition that has impacted more than 30,000 young women of color.

Mr. Jackson recently celebrated 60 years in broadcasting and, for than twenty years, has hosted the Hal Jackson's "Sunday Classics" on WBLS in New York City and was the first African American inducted into the Broadcast Hall of Fame. Included among Hal's numerous awards and honors, are: the 2003 Rhythm & Blues Foundation Broadcast Pioneer Award, the 2003 New York Achievement in Radio Award for Lifetime Achievement and the NAACP Image Award. He has also received five Presidential Citations from Presidents Clinton, Bush, Kennedy, Eisenhower, Franklin Roosevelt and Harry Truman.

# John H. Johnson

John H. Johnson, founder, publisher, chairman and CEO of the Johnson Publishing Company Inc., Chicago, Ill., the largest black-owned publishing company in the world, with a circulation of 1.7 million and a monthly readership of 11 million has been called the most influential African-American publisher in American history. He has been awarded the Presidential Medal of Freedom, the highest honor the nation can bestow on a citizen, from President Bill Clinton in 1996.

Johnson was born a descendant of slaves in Arkansas City, Ark., in 1918. His mother, Gertrude Johnson Williams, worked as a domestic and a levee cook to raise the money to move to the family to Chicago. At the time, no high schools for blacks existed in Arkansas City. Johnson repeated the eighth grade in Arkansas rather than end his education. In Chicago, Johnson graduated from DuSable High School where he was on the honor roll, served as senior class president, editor of the newspaper, and yearbook editor. He later became editor of the Supreme Life Insurance Company newsletter.

In 1942, Johnson started Johnson Publishing and published the first issue of Negro Digest with a $500 loan against his mother's furniture. Through the years, the company evolved to include a book division and also publishes Jet magazine, the number one black news weekly with a readership of over eight million. Johnson Publishing employs more than 2,600 people with sales of over $388 million. The company also owns Fashion Fair Cosmetics, the number one makeup and skin care company for women of color around the world and Supreme Beauty products, hair care for men and women. Johnson Publishing is also involved in television production and produces the Ebony Fashion Fair, the world's largest traveling fashion show, which has donated over $47 million to charity. The show visits more than 200 cities in the United States, Canada and the Caribbean.

In 1971, Johnson Publishing moved to its new 11-story headquarters on Chicago's fashionable Michigan Avenue, becoming the first African American-owned business to be located in the Loop. In 1982, John H. Johnson was the first African-American named to the Forbes' list of the 400 wealthiest Americans.

# Robert L. Johnson

Robert L. Johnson is the founder, chairman and chief executive officer of Black Entertainment Television (BET), a subsidiary of Viacom and the leading African American-owned and operated media and entertainment company in the United States. BET has enjoyed extraordinary financial and strategic success since its inception in 1980.

The core BET Network has pioneered an entire genre in television, with its 24-hour programming that targets African-American consumers that now reaches more than 65 million U.S. homes and more than 90% of all Black cable households. In 1998, Johnson established BET Pictures and BET Arabesque Films to produce and market African American-themed film releases, documentaries and made for TV movies. BET has also leveraged its brand identity into new businesses outside the cable industry with direct ownership of BET Arabesque Books (African-American romance novels written by African-American authors).

Robert L. Johnson is a graduate of the University of Illinois and holds a master's in International Affairs from the Woodrow Wilson School of Public and International Affairs at Princeton University. From 1976 to 1979, Johnson served as vice president of Government Relations for the National Cable & Telecommunications Association (NCTA), a trade association representing more than 1,500 cable television companies. Prior to joining the NCTA, Johnson was press secretary for the Honorable Walter E. Fauntroy, Congressional Delegate from the District of Columbia. He previously held positions at the Washington Urban League and the Corporation for Public Broadcasting.

Major awards received by Johnson include: 1997 Broadcasting & Cable Magazine's Hall of Fame Award; an NAACP Image Award; and the President's Award from the National Cable & Telecommunications Association.

# Quincy Jones

Quincy Delight Jones, Jr., known to his friends as "Q," was born on Chicago's South Side. When he was ten he moved, with his father and stepmother, to Bremerton, Washington, a suburb of Seattle. He first fell in love with music when he was in elementary school. At 18, Quincy won a scholarship to Berklee College of Music in Boston, but dropped out abruptly when he received an offer to go on the road with bandleader Lionel Hampton. By 1956, Quincy Jones was performing as a trumpeter and music director with the Dizzy Gillespie band on a State Department-sponsored tour of the Middle East and South America. Shortly after his return, he recorded his first albums as a bandleader in his own right for ABC Paramount Records.

In 1957, Quincy settled in Paris where he studied composition. Soon after, he formed his own big band, but concert earnings could not support a band of this size and the band dissolved, leaving its leader deeply in debt.

After a personal loan from Mercury Records head Irving Green helped resolve his financial difficulties, Jones went to work in New York as music director for the label. In 1964, he was named a vice-president of Mercury Records, the first African-American to hold such an executive position in a white-owned record company.

The company, in which Jones serves as co-CEO and chairman, encompasses multi-media programming for current and future technologies, including theatrical motion pictures and television. QDE also publishes *Vibe* magazine and produces the popular NBC-TV series *Fresh Prince of Bel Air*. At the same time, Jones runs his own record label, Qwest Records and is chairman and CEO of Qwest Broadcasting, one of the largest minority-owned broadcasting companies in the United States. He continues to produce hit records, among his best-selling albums are *Back on the Block* and *Q's Jook Joint*. He is best-known as the producer of *Thriller*, the best-selling album of all time in the history of the music recording industry.

The all-time most nominated Grammy artist with a total of 76 nominations and 26 awards. His life and career were chronicled in 1990 in the critically acclaimed Warner Bros. film *Listen Up: The Lives of Quincy Jones*.

## Tom Joyner

Tom Joyner earned the nickname "The Fly Jock" and "The Hardest Working Man in Radio" by working long hours and flying between his morning job (in Dallas, Texas) and afternoon job (in Chicago, Illinois) every weekday for years.

One of two sons, Joyner grew up in the town of Tuskegee, Alabama, where his mother was a secretary for the military and his father served as a Tuskegee Airman. Tom actively fought for civil rights. Following a protest at a local radio station that refused to play "black" music, Tom convinced the manager to give him a position there.

Joyner graduated from Tuskegee Institute, where he earned a Bachelor's degree in Sociology and immediately began his career in radio. He started at WRMA (an AM station in Montgomery, Alabama). After breaking onto the airwaves there, he worked his magic at WLOK (an AM station in Memphis, Tennessee), KWK (an AM station in St. Louis, Missouri), and KKDA (an FM station in Dallas, Texas).

Eventually, Joyner moved to Chicago, where he worked on radio stations WJPC (FM), WGCI (FM), WVON (AM) and WBMX (FM) and caused a whirlwind of excitement on urban radio.

In the mid 1980's, was offered the MORNING drive time position at KKDA (Dallas, Texas) by one company and the AFTERNOON Disc Jockey position at WGCI (Chicago, Illinois). Any normal human would have chosen one position or the other—Tom Joyner chose to do BOTH! His plan was to fly thousands of miles everyday by airplane each day between Dallas and Chicago. He spent so much time in the air that he received the name "The Fly Jock". This commute and his rich on air style gained him national publicity and high ratings.

In 1994, Tom Joyner took his show to a new level. He convinced ABC Radio Networks that his show could work in syndication; and in 1994, The Tom Joyner Morning Show started with Tom Joyner at the helm.

The show is beamed into over 95 radio stations across the country each weekday, with over 10 million listeners. Tom Joyner was elected into the Radio Hall of Fame. He has received Billboard's "Best Urban Contemporary Air Personality" award and Impact Magazine's "Best DJ of the Year Award" was renamed "The Tom Joyner Award" because he received it so many times.

## Spike Lee

Spike Lee has established himself as one of Hollywood's most important and influential filmmakers in the past decade. In 1986, his debut film, the independently produced comedy, *She's Gotta Have It*, earned him the Prix de Jeunesse Award at the Cannes Film festival and set him at the forefront of the Black Wave in American Cinema.

*School Daze*, his second feature, not only proved highly profitable, but also launched the careers of several young African-American actors. Spike's timely 1989 film, *Do The Right Thing*, garnered an Academy Award nomination for Best Original Screenplay and Best Film & Director awards from the Los Angeles Film Critics Association. Lee's *Jungle Fever* and *Mo' Better Blues* were also critically well received, as were *Malcolm X* and *Clockers*.

Born in Atlanta, Georgia, Spike returned South from Brooklyn to attended Morehouse College. He continued his education at New York University's Tisch School of the Arts, where he received his Master of Fine Arts Degree in film production. Lee then founded 40 Acres and a Mule Filmworks and Musicworks. In addition. he has created two retail companies, Spike's Joint, based in the Fort Greene section of Brooklyn, where he has resided since childhood, and Spike's Joint West in Los Angeles.

In addition to his achievements in feature films, Lee has produced had directed numerous music videos, television commercials and short films. Additionally, Spike has authored six books on the making of his films.

## Byron Lewis

Byron Lewis is Founder, Chairman and Chief Executive Officer of UniWorld Group, Inc. In the 70's and 80's, he supervised advertising and media strategies for Kenneth Gibson's mayoral campaign, the first African-American Political Summit in Gary, Indiana; Rev. Jesse Jackson's first Presidential campaign, and the first on-site Black radio and press coverage of the 1976 Democratic and Republican Presidential National Conventions.

Lewis founded UniWorld Group in 1969 after searching unsuccessfully to find employment within the historically restricted mainstream advertising agencies, starting the company with $250,000 start-up grant, hard work and sheer optimism. Since that time, UniWorld has expanded into the nation's second-largest African American-owned firm. His agency has earned hundreds of millions of dollars in billings by helping Fortune 500 companies tailor spots to African-American audiences. UniWorld's clients have included AT&T, Colgate-Palmolive, Texaco, Ford and Kraft Foods.

Among UniWorld's clients are a number of the world's leading corporations, including: AT&T, Colgate-Palmolive, Burger King, Home Depot, Ford and Kraft Foods. In long-term partnerships with these clients, they enable their brands to effectively address ethnic audiences in a manner that is both culturally relevant and broadly appealing. UniWorld's work spans general market, African American and Hispanic campaigns. Under his UniWorld Film marketing division, Lewis created the Acapulco Black Film Festival.

## Ed Lewis

As chairman and CEO of Essence Communications Inc., a diversified, multi-million dollar corporation, Edward Lewis heads one of the most successful and diverse African American-owned communications companies in the U.S.

Lewis graduated from the University of New Mexico with a bachelor's degree in political science and international relations. He enrolled in the Georgetown University Law School, but left after one year to participate in the executive training program at First National City Bank in New York City. He further enhanced his business skills by taking courses at the Harvard University Business School. Lewis was well on his way to becoming a loan officer when his career took a dramatic turn after he attended a conference on African Americans in business, where he saw the potential for a fashion magazine for African American women. His rise to prominence began within six months when, in 1969, he left banking to co-found *Essence* magazine with Clarence O. Smith. The first issue of *Essence* was published in May of 1970, with a print run of just 50,000 copies.

*Essence* has evolved into one of the leading lifestyle magazines for African American women, with a paid circulation of one million and a readership of 7.5 million. In 1992, Lewis expanded his publishing realm with the acquisition of Income Opportunities; three years later, he entered into a joint venture to publish Latina, the first bilingual lifestyle magazine that exclusively addresses the interests of Hispanic women in the U.S.

Since its inception, Essence Communications has appeared on all 25 listings of Black Enterprise's Top 100 Black firms. In 1997, Lewis was named chairman of the Magazine Publishers of America, the industry association for consumer magazines. He became the first African American to lead this trade group, which represents over 700 magazines.

## Reginald Lewis

Growing up in a middle class Baltimore neighborhood, Lewis won a football scholarship to Virginia State College (now Virginia State University), graduating with a degree in economics in 1965. He graduated from Harvard Law School in 1968. After working at several law firms, Lewis opened TLC Group, a venture capital firm. In 1987 Lewis bought Beatrice International Foods for $985 million, and created TLC Beatrice, a snack food, beverage, and grocery store conglomerate that was the largest African American-owned and African American-managed business in the U.S. At its peak in 1996, TLC Beatrice had sales of $2.2 billion and was number 512 on *Fortune* magazine's list of 1,000 largest companies. Lewis was also a prominent philanthropist. His 1992 gift to Harvard Law School was the largest single donation the school had received and created the Reginald F. Lewis Fund for International Study and Research. After his death, his half-brother and former football player Jean S. Fugett took over the company.

## Tony Rose

Tony Rose is the Founder, Publisher and CEO of Amber Communications Group, Inc. (ACGI). Amber Books Publishing, the corporation's first imprint, was founded in 1998 and experienced phenomenal growth in a niche market that established them as the nation's largest African-American publisher of self-help and career-guide books for African-Americans in the World. Based in Phoenix, Arizona and New York City, ACGI's imprints include: Amber Books, Busta Books, Colossus Books, Ambrosia Books and Amber/Wiley Books.

Rose was born in Roxbury (Boston), Massachusetts and raised on welfare in a single parent home in the Whittier Street Housing Projects. He began his first business as a newspaper boy at the age of six. Rose attended the University of Massachusetts and the University of California in Los Angeles, graduating with a B.A. in Journalism and English Literature.

In the 80's and 90's, Rose founded and operated Solid Platinum Records and Productions, where he managed and produced, among the company's numerous acts, Prince Charles and the City Beat Band. He also recorded his and several other international acts, which included New Kids on the Block, in his Boston and New York City-based Hit City Recording Studios.

Solid Platinum Records and Productions held production deals with Virgin records, Atlantic Records and SONY Records; and was the first African-American production company to have a production deal with Virgin Records. In 1996, he sold his music business to Unidisc Productions in Montreal and EMI Music Publishing in the United Kingdom.

Determined to make a difference to the people of America's inner cities, Rose acted upon his vision of selling self-help books that offer information and knowledge, specifically written by and for African-Americans and invested a portion of his earnings in Amber Books Publishing.

Rose is one of less than seven major independent African-American book publishers in the United States. Under his guidance, ACGI has experienced tremendous growth and international recognition, resulting in hundreds of thousands of books being sold.

ACGI has co-publishing/imprint deals for six books with John Wiley & Sons, Inc. and has secured licensing for nine titles with Black Expressions Book Club, the nation's largest African-American book club.

Tony Rose has been highly recognized by his peers for his vision and a unique approach to book publishing that has opened many doors and arenas for those up-and-coming book authors and book publishers. He has won numerous publisher and press awards, including: *The 2003 Black-Board Bestseller's African-American Publisher of the Year Award, the 2003 American Library Association "Reluctant Reader" Award* and *The Chicago Black Bookfair and Conference Independent Publisher / Press Award.*

## Russell Simmons

Russell Simmons, hip-hop pioneer, is the founder of Rush Communications, one of the largest African-American-owned media firms. In 1983 Simmons formed Def Jam Recordings, the core of Rush, which launched the careers of artists such as the Beastie Boys, LL Cool J, Run-DMC, and

Public Enemy. Simmons later sold Def Jam to Universal Music to focus on media production ("OneWorld" magazine, Def Poetry Jam) and various product lines (DefCon3 energy soda, i90 cellphones). In addition, the Rush Philanthropic Arts Foundation brings arts education to inner-city kids.

Russell Simmons didn't invent rap, but he mainstreamed it. He is, perhaps more than any other individual, responsible for the music's astonishing success. Like rock 'n' roll itself, rap was supposed to be a fad; but twenty years later, the genre represents the single most significant development in pop culture in the past two decades. In 1985, before Russell Simmons had even a single gold record on his wall, he and his partner, Rick Rubin, who together owned the fabled Def Jam record label, signed a production deal with CBS Records for $600,000. That kind of money is pocket lint to Simmons now. Recently, he sold the label that he built for $100 million.

The same year that Simmons, who is nicknamed Rush, signed the deal with CBS, the budding rap impresario produced a Hollywood movie called "Krush Groove", which starred rap group Run-D.M.C., Rick Rubin and Blair Underwood in Simmons' place. The $3 million movie returned $20 million.

Simmons was soon at the helm of Rush Communications, a conglomerate that includes a record label (Def Jam), a management company (Rush Artist Management), a clothier (Phat Farm), a movie production house (Def Pictures), television shows ("Def Comedy Jam" and "Russell Simmons' Oneworld Music Beat"), a magazine (Oneworld) and an advertising agency (Rush Media Co.).

## Tavis Smiley

The third oldest of ten children, Tavis Smiley grew up near an Air Force base in Kokomo, Indiana, where his father was a master sergeant and his mother a Pentecostal minster.

Smiley attended Indiana University, where the death of a classmate at the hands of the police first made him aware of the issues facing the African American community. He spent a semester as an intern in the office of Los Angeles Mayor Tom Bradley and graduated from Indiana University with a degree in law and public policy.

He returned to Los Angeles and worked as an adviser to the City Council president. Soon after, Smiley started the Smiley Report, a 60-second radio news commentary. The report's popularity earned Smiley his own television talk show on Black Entertainment Television, BET Tonight with Tavis Smiley. In April 2001, thousands of Smiley's viewers were outraged when BET terminated his contract.

Tavis Smiley had become known as Black America's favorite talk show host, honored with the NAACP Image Award for Best "News, Talk or Information Series" for three consecutive years.

In addition to hosting The Tavis Smiley Show from NPR (a first for an African American), Smiley currently offers political commentary on the Tom Joyner Morning Show and is a contributing editor for USA Weekend magazine. He is also a correspondent for CNN and an ABC-TV special correspondent for Good Morning America and Primetime Thursday. His newest venture is a late night television show—Tavis Smiley—is the first program in the history of PBS to broadcast from the West Coast. Tavis Smiley features a unique mix of news and pop culture to combine for one thought-provoking and entertaining program. It's a hybrid of news, issues and entertainment, featuring interviews with newsmakers, politicians, celebrities and real people.

Tavis is the author of five books, including *How to Make Black America Better*, and is publisher of The Smiley Report newsletter. In 1999, he founded the Tavis Smiley Foundation, a nonprofit organization, whose mission is to encourage, empower and enlighten African-American youth. Smiley's success has brought him numerous awards and honors, including a Congressional Black Caucus Harold Washington Award and the NAACP President's Image Award.

## Madame C. J. Walker

Sarah Breedlove Walker, known as Madame CJ Walker, was the first African American woman millionaire in America, known not only for her hair straightening treatment and her salon system, which helped other African Americans to succeed, but also her work to end lynching and gain women's rights. The Madame C.J. Walker Manufacturing Company produced and distributed a line of hair and beauty preparations for black women, including conditioners to ease styling, stimulate hair growth, and cure common scalp ailments, as well as an improved metal comb for straightening curly hair.

Madame CJ Walker was born in 1867 in poverty-stricken rural Louisiana. The daughter of former slaves, she was orphaned at the age of seven, then Walker and her older sister survived by working in the cotton fields of Delta and Vicksburg, Mississippi. She married at age fourteen and her only daughter was born in 1885. After her husband's death two years later, she traveled to St. Louis to join her four brothers who had established themselves as barbers. Working as a laundrywoman, she managed to save enough money to educate her daughter, and became involved in activities with the National Association of Colored Women.

During the 1890s, when Sarah began to suffer from a scalp ailment that caused her to lose some of her hair, she experimented with a variety of homemade remedies and products made by another African-American woman entrepreneur, Annie Malone. In 1905 Sarah became a sales agent for Malone and moved to Denver, where she married Charles Joseph Walker.

She founded her own business and began selling Madam Walker's Wonderful Hair Grower, a scalp conditioning and healing formula. To promote her products, she embarked on an exhausting sales drive throughout the South and Southeast, selling her products door to door, giving demonstrations and working on sales and marketing strategies. In 1908, she opened a college in Pittsburgh to train her "hair culturists."

Eventually, her products formed the basis of a thriving national corporation employing at one point over 3,000 people. Her Walker System, which included a broad offering of cosmetics, licensed Walker Agents, and Walker Schools offered meaningful employment and personal growth to thousands of Black women.

Having amassed a fortune in fifteen years, this pioneering businesswoman died at the age of 52. Her prescription for success was perseverance, hard work, faith in herself and in God, "honest business dealings" and of course, quality products.

## Terrie Williams

Terrie Williams opened the doors to the Terrie Williams Agency in 1988 by signing Eddie Murphy and Miles Davis as her first two clients. Over the years The Agency handled the biggest names in entertainment, sports, business and politics.

Terrie is one of the country's most highly sought-after speakers, and has shared her own brand of success and personal development strategies with numerous Fortune 500 companies, and organizations such as New York University's Continuing Education Program, the New School for Social Research, as well as The National Hockey League, The National Basketball Association and The National Football League

In September 1994 Warner Books published Terrie's *The Personal Touch: What You Really Need to Succeed in Today's Fast-Paced Business World. The Personal Touch* has been used as a guide at business workshops, lectures and corporate success courses given across the country. Terrie is also the author of *The Personal Touch* for teenagers tentatively titled *Stay Strong: Life Lessons for Teens* published by Scholastic and an inspirational, self-help book called *A Plentiful Harvest: Creating Balance and Harmony Through Seven Living Virtues* on Warner Books.

A licensed social worker, Terrie also counsels professional athletes, at-risk youth and non-profit organizations that work with young adults and children and has established the Stay Strong Foundation, a mentoring program for teens.

In 1998 Terrie donated a collection of her business and personal papers to Howard University's Moorland-Spingarn Research Center, the center's first gift of material specific to the public relations field. Terrie is the first and only woman of color to be so honored in the 31-year history to receive The New York Women in Communications Matrix Award in Public Relations.

## Oprah Winfrey

Born in Kosciusko, Mississippi, Oprah Winfrey was reared by her grandmother on a farm where she "began her broadcasting career" by learning to read aloud and perform recitations at the age of three. From age six to 13, she lived in Milwaukee with her mother. After suffering abuse and molestation, she ran away and was sent to a juvenile detention home at the age of

13, only to be denied admission because all the beds were filled. As a last resort, she was sent to Nashville to live under her father's strict discipline. Vernon Winfrey saw to it that his daughter met a midnight curfew, and he required her to read a book and write a book report each week.

Oprah Winfrey's broadcasting career began at age 17, when she was hired by WVOL radio in Nashville, and two years later signed on with WTVF-TV in Nashville as a reporter/anchor. She attended Tennessee State University, where she majored in Speech Communications and Performing Arts.

In 1976, she moved to Baltimore to join WJZ-TV news as a co-anchor, and in 1978 discovered her talent for hosting talk shows when she became co-host of WJZ-TV's "People Are Talking," while continuing to serve as anchor and news reporter.

In January 1984, she came to Chicago to host WLS-TV's "AM Chicago," a faltering local talk show. In less than a year, she turned "AM Chicago" into the hottest show in town. The format was soon expanded to one hour, and in September, 1985 it was renamed "The Oprah Winfrey Show."

Seen nationally since September 8, 1986, "The Oprah Winfrey Show" became the number one talk show in national syndication in less than a year.

Before America fell in love with Oprah Winfrey the talk show host, she captured the nation's attention with her poignant portrayal of Sofia in Steven Spielberg's 1985 adaptation of Alice Walker's novel, *The Color Purple.* Her love of acting and her desire to bring quality entertainment projects into production prompted her to form her own production company, HARPO Productions, Inc., in 1986. Today, HARPO is a formidable force in film and television production. Based in Chicago, HARPO Entertainment Group includes HARPO Productions, Inc., HARPO Films and HARPO Video, Inc. In October, 1988, HARPO Productions, Inc. acquired ownership and all production responsibilities for "The Oprah Winfrey Show" from Capitol Cities/ABC, making Oprah Winfrey the first woman in history to own and produce her own talk show.

Oprah is co-founder of Oxygen Media, which was formed in November 1998 along with fellow founders Geraldine Laybourne, Marcy Carsey, Tom

Werner, Caryn Mandabach. Oxygen Media includes the Oxygen Network, a women's cable network that launched on February 2, 2000 and is currently available in 48 million homes across the country.

In April 2000, Oprah and Hearst Magazines introduced *O, The Oprah Magazine,* a monthly magazine that has become one of today's leading women's lifestyle publications.

In 2001, Oprah and Harpo Productions announced the creation of the new, daily, syndicated series, *Dr. Phil,* featuring life strategist Dr. Phil McGraw, Ph.D., who appeared as a regular guest on *The Oprah Winfrey Show* from 1998 through 2002. The show, which has ranked number two since its debut on September 16, 2002, is produced by Paramount Domestic Television and distributed in national syndication by King World Productions and globally by CBS Broadcast international.

When *Forbes* magazine published its list of America's billionaires for the year 2003, it disclosed that Oprah Winfrey was the first African-American woman to become a billionaire.

As a philanthropist, Oprah includes numerous causes. The Oprah Winfrey Foundation was established to support the inspiration, empowerment, education and well-being of women, children and families around the world. Through this private charity, Oprah has contributed millions of dollars towards providing a better education for underserved students who have merit but no means. She is also the recipient of countless awards and honors, including: 39 Daytime Emmy Awards and The National Academy of Television Arts & Sciences' Lifetime Achievement Award and In 1998, *Time* Magazine named her one of the 100 most influential people of the 20th Century.

## Sylvia Woods

In August of 1962 Sylvia Woods purchased the restaurant, which then was only a small luncheonette, from her boss. Fifty years later, Sylvia's has become the landmark of 126th St. and Lenox Avenue and the one place where everyone knows they can get a taste of authentic Southern Soul food.

Growing up as an only child in Hemingway, South Carolina, Sylvia was raised by two widows, her mother and grandmother. Her mother never had an education, but she owned a farm and was a midwife. After moving to New York from South Carolina, Sylvia and her husband Herbert raised their four children in a five-room apartment on 131st St. in Harlem.

Cooking homemade food, based on the recipes used by her mother and grandmother, Sylvia, with the support of her late husband, established a soul food empire; but in 1962, she could not even conceive of the success of her decision. In order to purchase the luncheonette, Sylvia's mother agreed to mortgage her family farm and gave her $18,000.

Sylvia's is a family business where most of her four children and 18 grand-children began working in the restaurant in their early teens. She has franchises in Kennedy Airport, New York and Atlanta; and her food can also be purchased at most supermarkets, in containers and bottles packed in her plant in New Jersey.

# Index

# ORDER FORM

## WWW.AMBERBOOKS.COM
### African-American Self Help and Career Books

Fax Orders:            480-283-0991      Postal Orders: Send Checks & Money Orders to:
Telephone Orders:    480-460-1660      Amber Books Publishing
Online Orders: E-mail: Amberbks@aol.com      1334 E. Chandler Blvd., Suite 5-D67
Phoenix, AZ 85048

_____ *How to Be an Entrepreneur and Keep Your Sanity*
_____ *Fighting for Your Life*
_____ *The House that Jack Built*
_____ *Langhorn & Mary: A 19th American Century Love Story*
_____ *The African-American Woman's Guide to Great Sex, Happiness, & Marital Bliss*
_____ *The Afrocentric Bride: A Style Guide*
_____ *Beautiful Black Hair: A Step-by-Step Instructional Guide*
_____ *How to Get Rich When You Ain't Got Nothing*
_____ *The African-American Job Seeker's Guide to Successful Employment*
_____ *The African-American Travel Guide*
_____ *Suge Knight: The Rise, Fall, and Rise of Death Row Records*
_____ *The African-American Teenagers Guide to Personal Growth, Health, Safety, Sex and Survival*
_____ *Aaliyah—An R&B Princess in Words and Pictures*
_____ *Wake Up and Smell the Dollars! Whose Inner City is This Anyway?*
_____ *How to Own and Operate Your Home Day Care Business Successfully Without Going Nuts!*
_____ *The African-American Woman's Guide to Successful Make-up and Skin Care*
_____ *How to Play the Sports Recruiting Game and Get an Athletic Scholarship:*
_____ *Is Modeling for You? The Handbook and Guide for the Young Aspiring Black Model*

Name:_____

Company Name:_____

Address:_____

City:_____State:_____Zip:_____

Telephone: (_____) _____ E-mail:_____

        For Bulk Rates Call: **480-460-1660**      **ORDER NOW**

| | | |
|---|---|---|
| How to be an Entrepreneur | $14.95 | ❑ Check ❑ Money Order ❑ Cashiers Check |
| Fighting for Your Life | $14.95 | ❑ Credit Card: ❑ MC ❑ Visa ❑ Amex ❑ Discover |
| The House That Jack Built | $16.95 | |
| Langhorn & Mary | $25.95 | |
| Great Sex | $14.95 | CC#_____ |
| The Afrocentric Bride | $16.95 | |
| Beautiful Black Hair | $16.95 | Expiration Date:_____ |
| How to Get Rich | $14.95 | **Payable to:** |
| Job Seeker's Guide | $14.95 |     Amber Books |
| Travel Guide | $14.95 |     1334 E. Chandler Blvd., Suite 5-D67 |
| Suge Knight | $21.95 |     Phoenix, AZ 85048 |
| Teenagers Guide | $19.95 | |
| Aaliyah | $10.95 | **Shipping:**     $5.00 per book. Allow 7 days for delivery. |
| Wake Up & Smell the Dollars | $18.95 | **Sales Tax:** Add 7.05% to books shipped to Arizona addresses. |
| Home Day Care | $12.95 | |
| Successful Make-up | $14.95 | **Total enclosed: $**_____ |
| Sports Recruiting: | $12.95 | |
| Modeling: | $14.95 | |